graceful living

graceful living

a course in the appreciation

of the sacraments

by john fearon, o. p.

the newman press
westminster, maryland
1955

Nihil obstat: EDWARD A. CERNY, S.S., D.D.
     Censor Librorum

Imprimatur: FRANCIS P. KEOUGH, D.D.
     Archbishop of Baltimore

September 6, 1955

The *nihil obstat* and *imprimatur* are official declarations that a book or pamphlet is free of doctrinal and moral error. No implication is contained therein that those who have granted the *nihil obstat* and *imprimatur* agree with the opinions expressed.

All quotations from the New Testament are taken from the Confraternity of Christian Doctrine edition, 1947.

There are many books in English about the sacraments; this is going to be another. It is not likely that any one man is going to write a book to end all books about the sacraments. Each author contributes the fruit of his thoughts in the hope that some readers will be enlightened by what he writes. No writer says everything, no reader understands everything. So the more books that are written on the subject, and the more books that are read on the subject, the more likely it is that more people will know more about the sacraments.

Knowing about the sacraments is important when it comes to leading a fruitful Christian life. Of course, it is possible to get by as a Catholic and know very little about the sacraments—merely intending what the Church intends. Baptized as a baby, married in a daze, and anointed in a coma—such might be the lot of many who will rub shoulders with the saints in heaven for all eternity. But the sacraments were not designed for the unconscious, the dazed, and the comatose; they were designed for people who are wide awake to what is going on. A man might well never reflect on what happened to him when he was born, never speculate on what it will be like to die, never stay awake during a sermon or a scintillating conversation, or never feel a flutter of feeling before a sunset or at the opera. It might well be, but such a man is a bit of a vegetable; he is not leading a full human life.

A Catholic can be baptized and anointed while unconscious; confirmed, married, or ordained while in a fog; confess and communicate while distracted; hardly ever give a thought to the theology of the sacraments, and still slip through the pearly gates. But that sort of Catholic is missing a lot in life; he is surviving on crackers and water when the eats and drinks are on the house.

In the sacraments God is dealing with the human soul, the human mind, and the human heart. When God deals with creatures He deals with them in a way that is suited to their natures, with cats in a feline way and with men in a human way. Men are typically human when they are conscious and alert to what is going on, not when they are befuddled and asleep. God likes to deal with us at our conscious and intelligent best. In the sacraments He is giving us life, He is teaching us, He is making love to us, He is forgiving us, and He is strengthening us. In those moments, to the degree that it is possible, we ought to be at our intelligent best. You cannot really enrich the life of a vegetable with music.

Reading and studying the theology of the sacraments is one way to enrich one's sacramental life; that is why, when it comes to books on the subject, the more the merrier. This book is going to be borrowed largely from and based almost completely on Saint Thomas Aquinas' treatment of the sacraments in the *Summa Theologica,* one of the finest theology books on the market. That will deprive this work of originality, but in theology originality is undesirable in one reluctant to run afoul of the Holy Office. As a matter of fact, all books on the sacraments for many centuries past look to Saint Thomas for their inspiration, doctrine, and footnotes. This book is merely going to try to get across a few fundamental Thomistic concepts, and add a few commonplace analogies and some practical reflections. Like all authors who try to elaborate on the *Summa Theologica,* this author says if you dislike anything in this book, please do not blame Saint Thomas.

J. F.

Los Angeles, California
March, 1955

contents

graceful living

signs of life

Saint Thomas begins what he has to say about the sacraments by establishing the fact that they are signs. That is a very fine beginning because this business of signs is the key idea to an understanding of the sacraments, and it is only right that the key idea should be put at the beginning. Suppose you have before you on the table a portrait of your mother. There are two things you can say about the portrait. You can say, "That is my mother, as fine a Christian woman as ever dipped her hand in holy water. And it's a fine likeness too." Or you can say, "That is a piece of canvas covered with oil paint." In the first instance you are talking about the portrait as a sign. You can attribute to it the thing signified and call it mother. You can say that it is a good sign or a bad sign, a good portrait or a bad portrait. In the second instance you are talking about the portrait as a thing, disregarding the fact that it is a sign. It is important to know just what aspect of the portrait is under consideration and it is important to keep those aspects clearly distinct, or you end up saying that mother is but a piece of canvas smeared all over with oil paint.

A theologian is interested in the sacraments only insofar as they are signs. He leaves the chemical analysis of baptismal water to the chemist; for him the meaning of baptismal water is not H_2O. Hence the key to understanding what a theologian has to say about the sacraments is to remember that he is talking about them as signs.

There are many different kinds of signs. If you step on a woman's foot in the bus and she begins to get red in the face, it is a sign that you have earned her displeasure. If the bank returns your checks with a note that you are overdrawn, it is a sign that your funds are exhausted. Words, whether they are written or spoken, are always signs. If the lady in the bus tells me in strong terms that I am clumsy it is just as much a sign of her displeasure as is the red face. There are many different kinds of signs but they all have this in common: they lead us to a knowledge of something beyond themselves. The sudden flush of red in the woman's face is an entirely different thing from the red on the wall of a barn. A sign is a vehicle for communicating thoughts. Signs may be made of colors or letters or syllables; they may be effects, as smoke is the effect of fire; they may be causes, as fire is the cause of heat; they may be likenesses, as the portrait is a likeness of mother; but they are all addressed to the mind of man and lead to a knowledge of something beyond themselves. In all these ways the sacraments are signs. They are a cause of grace telling us what is happening to the soul; they are an effect of the passion and death of Jesus, reminding us of the source of grace; they are likenesses, as the separate consecration of the bread and wine is like to the separation of body and blood in the death of Jesus. But the important thing to remember is that as signs they are filled with meaning; they are addressed to the mind of man; they are Christ speaking to us.

Consider that phrase for a minute—they are Christ speaking to us. Actually only a few of the sacraments employ the words of Christ—Baptism for example. But there are more ways of speaking than by words. We often say that actions speak louder than words. Gestures, a raised eye-brow, a kiss, a frown—all these things speak volumes. And they are signs. Take, for example, an artist, a composer, a poet, or a painter: he is filled with a glimpse of beauty, an inspiration we usually call it, which he wants to communicate to us. He uses stone, or sound, or paint, but he uses them as signs to communicate something of his inspiration to us. Christ speaking to us in the sacraments is like an artist speaking, a master artist.

Suppose a parent or a teacher or a preacher

wants to promote virtue in a child or a pupil or a parishioner; and suppose that virtue is chaste love. The parent, the teacher, and the preacher are limited for the most part to explaining the values of this virtue in order to make it attractive; they appeal to reason. But the artist has this advantage: he appeals to more than reason; he appeals to mind and heart and feeling. With a poem, or a picture, or a bit of music he can propose an ideal of chaste love, rich in beauty, which appeals to heart and feeling as well as reason. An artist can make a more profound impression than a teacher; yet teachers and artists alike are limited in their efforts. Simple exposure to lectures and to music does not invariably make people good. In moving the mind and heart and feelings of man, the sacraments have the persuasive power of truth that a teacher has, the attractive power of beauty that the artist has, but over and above all this they have the power of God Himself to move the mind and heart of man both freely and infallibly. Indeed, the sacraments are signs that are meaningful like words, beautiful like works of art, but over and above this, effective like the right hand of God. Being meaningful they inform, being beautiful they charm, and being effective they sanctify.

Schools and radio stations have programs in music appreciation. Educators know very well that the masterpieces of great musical geniuses like Bach and Beethoven are a tremendous source of deep, noble, and pleasant human experiences for those who can appreciate them. They also know that, by and large, the music on the hit parade and the singing commercials are the people's choice. Nevertheless, music appreciation programs are designed to enable more people to experience the profound and moving pleasure of symphony and opera. Deems Taylor has been quite successful in this type of work. By explaining how the various masterpieces were produced, the suffering and the toil that went into them, how this or that composer had to feed fifteen children and work as a barber by day so that he could write his music by night, by explaining just what the artist is trying to convey and pointing out how he does it with the woodwinds or the drums or the strings, Deems Taylor has done much to help people appreciate the best in music. Basically, this book is going to be of the Deems Taylor variety, a course in the appreciation of the sacraments. By explaining the sufferings and toil that went into their production, by pointing out just what Christ is trying to do and how He goes about it, perhaps a fuller understanding of the sacraments may result, and, over and above that, a greater ability to experience more fully the effects these sacraments are supposed to evoke in the mind and heart.

The ordinary householder can walk into a dark room and announce, "Let there be light," flick the light switch, and the room lights up. However accurately our householder may quote the Book of Genesis, the procedure in the latter was quite different. In Genesis the existence of light depended totally on God. But the existence of light in the Jones' bed chamber is a more complicated, if less marvelous process. Jones flips the switch; so the existence of light depends on him. But the electrician installed the equipment, and when it fails he gets the blame; so the light must depend on him too. Furthermore, Thomas Edison invented the light bulb and hence deserves some credit for the light, not to mention the kindly God of nature who provides the forces that provide the electricity without which Jones would be in the dark.

When the priest pours a little water over the head of a baby and pronounces the words of Baptism, the soul of that child is sanctified and filled with the grace of God. When God created Adam, his soul was also sanctified and filled with grace in that very moment. The Baptism of Jones Junior in the local baptistry is less marvelous than the creation of Adam in the state of grace, but it is a good deal more complicated, just like the light in the Jones' bed-chamber. The sanctification of the child depends on the priest pouring the water and saying the words; it depends on God who is the source of all sanctity, and, to follow out the analogy, it depends on Christ, too, in somewhat the same way that a lighted room depends on Edison.

God is the source of sanctity and grace in a very special way. He is the adequate and principal cause of grace and He can sanctify a soul all by Himself without any help from anybody else, just as He made light by His authoritative word and created Adam in grace. At the other end of things, the priest is just a minister. He could pour water by the gallon and recite formulae in Latin, Greek and English. Except for the causality of God and Jesus, however, nothing would happen—somewhat the same way that Jones could flick his light switch until the spring broke and nothing would happen if there were no electricity or no genius like Edison. It might be well to mention that how good or bad the priest is does not make any difference in the effect of the sacraments, just as it does not make any difference whether Jones is drunk or sober when he flicks his light switch. The light goes on just the same.

Just as only a genius could invent the electric light, so too only Jesus could make a sacrament. Jesus is both God and man. Since grace and sanctity come from God as from a principal and adequate cause, Jesus, as God, can sanctify in any way He chooses. That part presents no problem. Just as He could have said, "Let there be light coming from a light bulb," and it would have happened, so too He could say, "Let there be grace coming through sacraments," and it did happen. No other man can speak with the authority of God the way Jesus can.

However, Jesus instituted the sacraments not only as God but also as man. As a man He merited the grace that comes to us through the sacraments. It was because His obedience to the Father in His sufferings and death, His love for the Father, His mercy towards us were so pleasing to the Father that God again poured out His grace and favor upon mankind. The sacraments bring grace because they are reminders of that passion and death. No one else's good deeds could have moved the Father thus. Hence no one else can arrange that God is going to utilize a special set of signs and symbols in pouring out His grace. No one else has that much influence with the Father.

Another thing to keep in mind is that the human nature of Jesus is an instrument of the Godhead, somewhat the way the hand is the instrument of the mind of man in writing a letter. Just as only the mind can move the hand, so too, only the hand can move the pen; or rather, only those pens write letters that are moved by hands. Since only the human nature of Jesus is conjoined to the Godhead in this special kind of union which makes Him the instrumental cause of all grace, only Jesus can pick the signs and symbols which shall be as the pen in His hand in writing the glory of God. Nobody else has what it takes to make a sacrament.

The reader might have guessed that, up to now, he has been given nothing more than an explanation of the catechism definition of a sacrament: a visible sign instituted by Christ to give grace. In order to round out the picture, it might be well to go into the idea that the sacraments give grace.

That the sacraments give grace is quite clearly

a matter of Catholic faith. After all, it is by the sacraments that we are incorporated into Christ and joined to the Mystical Body. Thus St. Paul writes, "For you are all the children of God through faith in Christ Jesus. For all you who have been baptized into Christ, have put on Christ" (Gal. 3:26–27). Since it is grace that makes us members of Christ, the sacraments must give grace. How they give it is a different question. When the priest pours the water and recites the formula, it is not a matter of presenting a symbol or sign to the Father who then pours grace into the infant soul all by Himself. In sanctifying mankind God uses the human nature of Christ as an instrument joined to the Godhead. A very inexact parallel to this is the way the mind uses the hand in writing. Furthermore, just as the hand uses the pen, so too Christ uses the sacraments. In other words, the sacraments are instruments, too, but not united to Christ the way His human nature is united to His divine nature. They are united to Christ only in the way a pen is united to a hand in the writing process. The grace comes ultimately from God, but passes through the human nature of Jesus and depends upon it. The grace of Christ, in turn, passes through the sacraments and somehow depends upon them. The passing-through process is just as real as water running through a pipe. And the dependence here is just as real as the dependence of a love letter upon the pen and upon the hand that guides the pen. As the theologians put it, the sacraments not only signify grace but somehow also contain it.

Fountain pens and love letters, tap water and lead pipes are very real and concrete things that are quite easy to imagine. Although it is impossible to conjure up a picture of grace in the imagination, grace is just as real as these things. The big difference is that grace is spiritual, not material. Many things are quite real though invisible, and hence unimaginable—electricity for example. By merely looking at a wire one cannot tell whether it is alive or dead. Picking it up in the hand usually dispels any doubts. If the wire is alive the result will be roughly equivalent to being kicked by a mule. Thus it is with spiritual things; we know that they are very real because they have very real effects. No surgeon has ever seen a soul, but without the soul he no longer has a patient. And no one has ever seen a virtue with the naked eye, but courage makes the difference between whether a man stands and fights or turns and runs; justice and love determine whether the members of a group live at peace or assault each other with lead pipes and butcher knives. Biochemists still have not figured out a chemical formula for the life of a carrot, but vegetables really do live. Now, grace is just as real as life and in many ways it is a kind of life. An animal, a rabbit for example, can grow and reproduce just like a carrot; it has all the life functions of the carrot, and more. Man has all of the life functions of vegetables and animals, and more. All of these life functions are real. Grace, in turn, adds yet another dimension to human life; it gives one a share in the divine life and makes a man similar to Christ. The baptized can say in truth, "I live now, not I, but Christ lives in me."

Grace is a word that covers a number of different realities. It can mean sanctifying grace which gives this new kind of life to the human soul. It can also refer to virtues, those permanent states of character that make such a great difference in a man's life—faith and hope and charity and courage. It also refers to that added push God gives which provides moving force and will power to do good and noble things in the kingdom of God—like dying for the faith or rolling out of bed for early Mass. When it is said that the sacraments give grace, the word can be taken in all these different senses. Of course, each sacrament gives a special grace, different from the graces that the other sacraments give. Just what that special grace is in each instance will appear later. All that is important now is to realize that grace is not a thin and airy thing like imaginary lace on an invisible curtain, but life and force and power. It is life, not so much like life as found in the mushroom or the dandelion, but more like life as found in the Son of God. Again grace is force and power, not of the sort that moves trains or blows up cities, but of the sort that changes death to life, that moves the mind and heart of man with sweet but majestic freedom and infallibility.

The sacraments are visible signs instituted by Christ to give grace. Comparing them to the artistic masterpieces of the classical geniuses of the past might just possibly engender a distasteful frown in those devoted to the crew-cut in these matters. Well and good! Not everybody has to like the masters. But regardless of considerations of preference, keep in mind the point about the sacraments that is being illustrated—that they are masterpieces of Christ Himself, beautiful, persuasive, and powerful.

chapter two

seven pillars of wisdom

An umpire has a hectic life. He prays at night that God might preserve him in honesty and justice. He drinks carrot juice in the morning that his eyesight might not fail him in his hour of need. During the game he calls them as he sees them. If his decisions favor the home team the home-town fans take it for granted; if they favor the visiting team the home-town fans start in with pop bottles and seat cushions. The umpire never gets to be a hero. Fans always have feelings.

In religion as in baseball, the fans also have feelings, even if they are not religious feelings. Thus some do not give God one iota of credit for the sacraments, while others consider the sacraments as beneath man's dignity and hence the product of a small-minded God who has a grudge against our kind.

The first mistake is usually described as modernistic, a description flattering enough if you are a modernist, like telling an elderly matron how young she looks. Some of the modernists dress up their position in the trappings of the history of religion. They find parallels between Baptism and the initiation ceremonies of other religions, and so on through the other sacraments. They conclude that there is nothing special about Baptism, no special reason for asserting its divine origin. Others dress the same argument in the trappings of psychology. They hold that these ceremonies fill some deep-felt need of human nature and hence are found in all religions. Of course they conclude that Baptism, like all the rest of the sacraments, is an invention of man to satisfy the requirements of his nature, somewhat the same way that eyeglasses and shoes are an invention of man. Like the home-town fans, they will not give the umpire any credit for a favorable decision.

Now the weakness of the modernist's position is not necessarily in history or in psychology. What is wrong with him is his logic. Just because two things are similar, it does not follow with necessity that they come from the same source. Similar cures come from Rochester, Minnesota, and from Lourdes, France, but that does not make the brothers Mayo divine. And just because the rites of pagan religions and Christianity are both congenial to the mind and heart of man it does not follow that they are both inventions of man. After all, God can be just as congenially disposed toward man's nature as man himself is. And as a matter of fact, one of the basic principles of Catholic theology is that God treats each creature in accord with its nature.

The second mistake about the sacraments is less enlightened, since it has little to support it either from logic or from psychology and history. But then it is a mistake made by proud men who generally are unenlightened. At first sight their argument always seems impressive. It goes something like this: "The relationship between God and man is very personal and very spiritual. To clutter up this relationship with institutionalized religion and prayer formulae and concrete ceremonies and rites is a hideous thing since it puts barriers between the soul and God. Sacraments and ceremonies and churches are not from God but from priestcraft, a noxious and parasitic growth upon the spirit." The way to argue practically with a man like that is to ask him how often he says his prayers. Of course, the relationship between God and man is personal and spiritual, but that does not mean that it is only spiritual. Man is a partner in that relationship and man is part animal even when he prays, as any monk who has thought about breakfast during his meditations or any nun who has nodded at her prayers will testify. What might be stumbling blocks for an angel are but stepping stones for man. A son's love for his father is personal and spiritual, but that does not mean that it is a sin for him to give his father a necktie on Father's Day.

Arguments for the over-all wisdom of having sacraments presuppose only two things: man as he really is, and God as He really is. There is no doubt about it—if there is any spiritual activity going on in the head and heart of man, some sort of sense experience is presupposed. This does not mean that a man cannot pray well without first whiffing incense or splashing in holy water. It means that in man body and soul are linked together and are continuous, and that the spirit cannot get along completely without the body any more than the body can get along without the soul. Incense might aggravate a man's hay fever and develop a prejudice in him against High Masses, but such a situation is not a refutation of the basic theory of the dependence of the soul upon the body. The sacramental system is founded on human nature and not on human allergies.

If you are going to treat a man as a man you are going to have to talk his language and you are going to have to take into account this dependence of the spiritual upon the corporal. Man has to be fed and talked to and slapped upon the back. This is just what God does in the sacraments. God is an all-wise and all-provident God. He made man the way he is and He treats man the way He made him. In His dealings with creatures God does not squeeze blood from turnips. Thus, in saving the nature He has made, God saves it in a way that is congenial to human nature. He provides His spiritual assistance in a way that can be seen and heard and felt. He provides for us sensible signs or sacraments. It is God's way to use our ways.

Another factor to be considered is man's fallen nature, a thing not a little embarrassing to the proud man. Christian theology holds, and always has held, that human nature as it now exists in the people who ride the buses, till the soil, and dig divots in our golf courses, is in a state of disrepair. By something like a process of heredity, much of the damage that Adam and Eve suffered in their original escapade of unfaithfulness to God has come down to us. Quite frequently people remain blandly oblivious of their shabby state, much like a whole county of one-legged men wherein the deformity passes unremarked.

The effects of original sin are sometimes referred to as a wound, like a razor slash upon the chin. The reason for this analogy is that the most obvious effect of original sin is a lack of integration or continuity in human nature, somewhat like the lack of continuity on the skin of the face after a rush job with a dull razor. Thoughts do not always follow reality; feelings do not always follow common sense; behavior does not always follow better judgment. Now, if you cut your chin with the razor you do not put the red medicine and adhesive plaster on the nose. The medicine goes where the wound is. Part of original sin in the original sinner, and part of original sin as it affects us, involves getting too enamored of the material things of sense. It might be apples or it might be bourbon, but it is the same kind of wound. And on the principle that a good doctor applies the medicine where the wound is, it follows logically and wisely that grace and salvation come to us through the material things of sense. If one would like to dig a little deeper into the figure of speech, it might be noted that the big thing about original sin was pride; and the only medicine for pride is humiliation. So the proud man's complaint that the sacraments are humiliating has a bit of truth in it. What is wrong with the complaint is not what it says but that it is a complaint.

A further criticism often heard from the same complainers, it might be mentioned, is that ablutions, anointings, and prayer formulae are a part of religion wherever and whenever it is found. But the fact that many of these ceremonies satisfy deep-felt needs in the human psyche proves that in a religion instituted by God such things should also be found. If God did not provide them in His religion men would be sure to tack them on, and it is not very likely that man would do as good a job of it. A wise and kindly God could hardly have done otherwise.

Up to now the burden of this chapter has been to establish that sacraments are a good thing. We can turn now to their exact number. It is true that one sacrament could do the work of all seven. Christ could have invented a one-sacrament system. Or He could have invented a system in which we would receive three a day like vitamin tablets and a different set for each day in the week. But somehow seven seems to be just the right number. Of course, some of them are received only once, as Baptism and Confirmation, while others are repeated as required or permitted, as the sacraments of Penance and Matrimony.

In setting up just seven sacraments, divine wisdom was taking care of the needs of man. One of the ways God takes care of our needs is by helping out our weaknesses and bolstering us up in our defects. A blind man with one leg and no teeth has defects, and if you are going to take care of him, the first thing you have to do is buy him a dog, a wooden leg, and dentures. The basic defects that are found in the children of Adam, taken both individually and in groups, total up to seven.

In the first place, the children of Adam are born without the sanctifying grace of God; or, to put it in other words, they are born in the state of original sin. This is a matter of an absence of life which is supplied by Baptism. New life in mankind is a delicate thing which has to be strengthened and perfected before it is ready for the blow-by-blow affair that life turns out to be. Hence, Confirmation was invented to strengthen and perfect the life of grace in the soul, so that a Christian would be ready for the struggle that living in a pagan environment involves. However, the life of grace is not just a life of battling with the enemies of grace, but fundamentally a matter of loving

God. And to nurture growth in this dimension God provides the Eucharist. Life is like a teeter-totter: either we grow in love or we are overwhelmed by the fascination of earthly distractions. And the best way to off-set the fascination of earthly distractions is to promote fascination for the all-good God. Yet, even with these helps, man still has a free will and a mind that is easily turned by worldly things. Consequently, it happens that quite a few men fall into serious sin even after they have received Communion; and to restore the life of grace after it has been destroyed by personal sins, the sacrament of Penance was invented. After floundering through the years, wasting opportunities and neglecting the things of the spirit, it is a rare soul that can face the business of dying in a stalwart Christian manner. To provide energy in that dread moment Christ provided the sacrament of Extreme Unction. In group living, one of the biggest needs is leadership. Holy Orders provides this. Finally, it might be noted that there are two sexes, and consequently families. Anybody who has reflected on this fact must have noticed, also, that the difficulties and problems of married life require a special kind of strengthening. The sacrament of Matrimony deepens love and provides what is required to be a good Christian parent. These needs will be explained at greater length later on. A glance at them now is enough to indicate that God has shown a thorough grasp of our infirmities. If any man now flounders in the creek of life it is because he left the paddle on shore.

God cares for us in the kingdom of heaven, not only by providing for our defects, but also by supplying what is needed for positive progress in grace. Viewing the sacraments from this positive side, seven still seems to be the best number. Remember that in the sacraments Christ is teaching us. A good teacher breaks the lesson up into easily digestible units. The mathematics teacher who crowds everything from simple addition to advanced calculus into one lecture generates nothing but confusion. Likewise the lessons of God are broken up into units with each sacrament being a lesson in itself. From birth until death, the sacraments are dispensed at moments in life when their lesson will be most impressive.

As previously mentioned, it was God's wish to deal with us in a human way, in a way congenial to our nature. And when God builds upon our nature and elevates us to that higher type of life which is the life of grace, He explains the process to us step by step in the sacraments. Nothing is more annoying than a dentist who assembles a formidable array of tools and commences work on the molars without explaining what he is going to do. God is not like that. At each phase He provides a simple explanation of what is going on in the soul so that we will not only have the life of grace but will know about it.

Because there is a certain likeness or parallel

between the life of grace and our natural human life, the sacramental system is broken up into units or lessons that correspond to the various phases and functions of our natural life. Some of these functions belong to man as an individual and some belong to man as a member of society. Thus, for example, digestion is a purely personal function and the arrest of a petty thief by a policeman is a social function.

Among the personal life functions to be found in everyone's life there are three basic ones which contribute to positive development. In the first place there is generation, which terminates in birth. Paralleling this in the supernatural life there is Baptism. The second of these functions is growth, whereby a baby develops into full, mature stature and strength. This function is supplied in the life of grace by Confirmation. The third function is called nutrition. It goes on constantly while man lives, supplying energy and building up wasted tissues. To this corresponds Holy Communion which is supposed to be repeated just like eating, and which builds up wasted strength and supplies energy for leading a holy Christian life. But the life of the spirit, like the life of the body, is subject to injury and sickness. In the life of the spirit this is sin and the weakness left behind by sin. Confession, like the extraction of a tooth, a surgical operation, or a dose of penicillin, removes the noxious force and thus cures the illness. After an illness or an operation there is a period of convalescence when the patient needs a special diet and sometimes special exercises to restore him to his pristine vigor. This is the function of Extreme Unction, which removes the remains of sin and prepares a man for final glory.

Broadly speaking, man may function as an official in society in two ways. He can either be a civic official handing out traffic tickets or passing laws and handing down decisions from a court-room bench, or he may be a parent. The sacrament of Holy Orders constitutes a man as an official in the social life of grace, for it is the priest and the bishop who teach, rule, and judge. The sacrament of Matrimony gives one the ability to function as a parent of good Christian offspring, somewhat the way sex, in the natural order, gives the ability to function in marriage as an institution of nature.

In this positive side of God's care for us, the wisdom of the Divine Teacher is evidenced. Later on these points will be explained more fully. At the present an over-all survey is all that is required to establish the fact that seven is just the right number of sacraments to have.

a string around the finger

Although the catechism says that sacraments are visible signs instituted by Christ to give grace, it seems legitimate enough to alter the definition just slightly and consider the sacraments as artistic masterpieces with Christ as the master artist. When it comes to applying this idea to a special sacrament like Baptism, the question arises as to just which art is involved. The necessity of the sacrament of Baptism becomes more clear if the divine artist is considered as engaged in the gentle but firm art of reminding, somewhat in the way that a string around the finger is a reminder.

Reminding is an art. It takes the right word, the right moment, and the right tone of voice. For example, the wife of a forgetful husband has a letter she wants him to mail. She can start in by giving him a lecture on the subject of his memory when he gets up in the morning. She can continue with further installments of the same while he shaves and eats his breakfast. She can make a great ceremony of presenting him with the invaluable epistle. She can bring up the subject again as he kisses her goodbye and heads for the front door. And finally she can shout after him on the subject of the letter in his coat pocket as he boards the bus down at the corner. This approach is calculated to bring about one of two effects. Either the husband will listen and he will stuff the letter in a city refuse can to express his chagrin, or he will ignore her tirade and be psychologically deaf to what she says, which means that the letter will be mailed only when she retrieves it from his coat pocket before his suit goes to the cleaners. And when it becomes a question of reminding him of her birthday or their wedding anniversary, the subject is still more delicate and requires still greater art. Without doubt, reminding is a firm but gentle art.

This approach to Baptism becomes quite clear when it is compared to circumcision in the Old Testament, which in many ways was parallel to Baptism although it was not a sacrament. When God first made His treaty with Abraham, He agreed that He would call the people of Abraham "my people." But one of the conditions of this treaty was that, among the children of Abraham, infant boys would be circumcised. God had no grudge against babies. It was only that circumcision was to be a reminder of the treaty; it was to remind the circumcised that although God had accepted them, they still stood in need of a Savior. And they stood in need of a Savior because original sin was still being passed on from generation to generation. Therefore, in picking out a sign that was to be a reminder, God picked on circumcision. A neat bit of reminding if ever there was one!

When the Savior came and the affairs between God and man were put on a new basis, Jesus did away with circumcision and instituted a new reminder, Baptism. After all, there was something new to be reminded about. Baptism is one of the two sacraments that Jesus made a great point of in His instructions. Furthermore, He Himself was baptized by John the Baptist who was a very famous figure. The dove appeared and the voice of the Father was heard from heaven. That was no unobtrusive ceremony; it was packed with importance. The importance came not because Jesus needed to be baptized, but because the sacrament of Baptism which was to follow was important.

Circumcision was a reminder that original sin was being passed on from generation to generation, but it did not point out that original sin was being taken away. It was a reminder that a Savior was needed. After the Savior had come, the signification of circumcision was empty and meaningless, like the time-table for a defunct railroad. In its place Christ put Baptism. Baptism points out that original sin is being taken away in virtue of the redemption brought about by the Savior who has already come.

The word "baptism" means a washing. Washing presupposes that something is dirty and needs washing. Suppose you have a guest in the house for dinner. His hands are indelicately smudged and the hour for dining draws near. Obviously any reference to hand washing is going to high-light the uncomfortable existence of the smudges. Two courses are open. The host can either peer with intent alarm and a tinge of disgust at the guest's dirty hands, or politely lead him past a washbasin on the way to the dining room. There is a very gentle art involved here. And Jesus, in insisting that we need to be washed if we are to enter the kingdom of heaven, is in that process reminding us that we first stand in need of washing, that we are from birth tainted with original sin. However, He brings the subject up with firmness but gentleness, with the masterful touch of a gentleman.

The washing is to be done with water. Actually there are a number of ways to go about washing: one could use milk, wine, oil or a modern detergent. Jesus insisted on water. Water does a much cleaner job of washing than milk, wine, or oil. It leaves behind no stickiness or odor. And the grace of Baptism does a clean job on the soul. Besides, the grace of Baptism was never meant to be a rich man's extravagance, but the common man's most necessary and most available spiritual endowment.

There are a number of other reasons, too, why

washing with clear water is an apt reminder. Clear water revives wilted plants. In washing away original sin, the grace of Baptism revives the wilted life in our souls, souls that without this refreshment would certainly fade away. Nearly everyone has had enough experience with gardening or house plants to know about wilted plants and water. Water not only refreshes plants, it also cleanses and refreshes the tired body. A body weary from being heavily burdened and overheated from toil responds, when one plunges into a swimming pool, much like the wilted flower. As a result of the effects of original sin, human nature becomes fatigued and tired from carrying the burden of concupiscence and the pride of life. All in all, washing with water was about as gentle and significant a reminder as one could imagine.

Washing with water had been used in religious rites before the time of Christ, so it was not a completely new invention. But, even in the external, sensible sign, Jesus did add something new—namely, the words, "I baptise you in the name of the Father, and of the Son and of the Holy Ghost." No one before had ever baptized in that name, not even John the Baptist. These words point out who is really cleansing the soul and in whose sight we now stand clean—the Triune God. At Christ's Baptism a voice from heaven thundered, "This is my beloved Son in whom I am well pleased." In our Baptism, too, we become clean and pleasing in the sight of the same God.

Suppose someone objected this way: "I can understand that it is nice for the church to have an initiation ceremony, just like the Boy Scouts or the Elks' Club, but it seems that the church is being entirely too technical about it when she says that one cannot get into heaven without it. God will not keep people out of heaven on a technicality."

As a matter of fact, Jesus can do without the sacrament everything that He does with it. From His point of view it is superfluous. Why then does He lay such stress on people having a little water poured over them and this special formula recited? The reason is because Baptism is a reminder and people need to be reminded. And Jesus does lay rather astonishing stress on how important this reminder, the sacrament of Baptism, is.

Take, for example, the business of inoculation. Being inoculated against small-pox is rather important. But in an average group of twenty people hardly two of them would know for sure whether they had been inoculated against small-pox or not. If it were announced over the radio that an epidemic of small-pox was ravaging the countryside, about eighteen of those people would be in a panic until they could find out for sure that they were immunized against the disease. The certitude of a certificate from a doctor and a scar are very comforting in times like that. So it is in the realm of the spirit. Whether or not we are children of God or labor under original sin is very important. At moments when the distractions of life subside, or the chips are down and a man begins to worry about how he stands with the heavenly Father, it makes considerable difference whether or not he has been accepted by God as an adopted son. Actually, if there were no sort of visible sign, a man could never know for sure about this sort of thing. All he would have to go by would be his feelings, and feelings are not a very reliable guide. To be left to rely on feelings in such moments, to be left in a state of doubt and uncertainty, would be most uncomfortable. But since Baptism is a visible sign, it is possible to actually have a certificate signed by the priest which states that we have been validly baptized. Most of us were baptized as babies and do not remember the ceremony. But the certificate verifies the fact with as much authority as we usually have in the affairs of life. A concrete reminder of divine acceptance is a great source of comfort.

Notice, too, what happens when a baby is born in the household. Beforehand there are showers. At the very moment itself everyone is enthusiastic, with the possible exception of the father who paces the hospital corridor with unspeakable anguish gnawing at his heart. Once the baby is born, friends and relatives crowd around a much pleased mother. From the look of satisfaction and accomplishment on the face of father, one would think that mother played a minor role in the affair. All and sundry crowd around and make enthusiastic and purring sounds and say how cute the infant is. Parents have a tendency to be very proud of their accomplishments. Babies always look so cute, at least to their parents. However, the fact that their cute little offspring must be baptized before it becomes a child of God is a good reminder of the insufficiency of human nature without Christ. Without Christ we cannot overcome original sin. God does not have to love the children of men just because they are human, or just because they are so cute and make such fine gurgling sounds, or look so much like uncle so-and-so. The children of men are loved by God only because the Father in His mercy deigns to accept them, and Baptism is the reminder of this.

With the custom of infant Baptism, this sacrament usually comes at a time when it should be most impressive. However, every priest knows what sort of conversation takes place after Baptism. There is a great scamper for cameras; there is a bit of handshaking. Perhaps someone remembers to slip an envelope into Father's hand with a knowing look. Perhaps a party follows; granted that it is a happy occasion. But, even with the reminder of Baptism, it is very seldom that a parent sighs with joy and announces that his child is now a child of God and that there is no need to worry about the future.

It is a comfort to be reminded that we have been baptized, though many years ago. It is important that, in the excitement which accompanies the birth of a child, the insufficiency of human nature to produce anything pleasing in God's sight without Christ should be recalled. But a reminder is necessary, too, lest we be ungrateful. One can readily see how it was important that the children of Abraham be reminded of original sin and that they needed a Savior. Without such a reminder they might well be like the household where there is someone sick. The doctor is sent for, but unless someone remembers the sickness and the fact that the doctor has been sent for, when the doorbell rings the doctor will be sent away. Expecting a Redeemer to come is important; but remembering to be grateful to a Redeemer who has come is more important still.

Really, it makes no difference if one forgets what day of the week it is. At most a business engagement will be missed or one will eat meat on Friday. It makes but little difference if we remember to mail letters or buy sauerkraut for supper. All these things might be forgotten and life will go on much the same. But remembering that we are baptized in the death of Christ is important. Remembering that we are children of God, not because we are cute, but because of Christ's passion and death is important. Remembering the insufficiency of human nature to do anything beautiful and pleasing in God's sight without the aid of Christ is important. Remembering these things makes all the difference in the world how a man shall live. It makes all the difference in the world in a man's attitude toward himself and toward God. And this attitude is the very stuff of which religion is made.

Baptism is such an artistic way of getting the point across. It is such a simple ceremony, and what is more available than water? Furthermore, in an emergency anyone can baptize. Any Christian who has reached the age of reason is old enough to know the formula. All that is required is that one know the formula, pour the water, and have the intention that the Church of Christ has in baptizing. The ceremony might be performed by an archbishop in a cathedral, a chaplain on the battlefield, a nurse in the maternity ward, or a missionary in the jungle. But it is the same ceremony. It is Christ's gentle but firm reminder that without Him no man is a child of God.

rebirth

In the third chapter of his Gospel Saint John rescues from oblivion a very interesting episode in the life of Jesus. This episode has to do with Nicodemus, who was among the wisest, most learned, and most influential men with whom Jesus dealt. With a certain quiet humor Jesus treats the great man to one of His simplest, shortest, and most illuminating explanations. Fortunately for us the subject that Jesus chose was Baptism.

One night, rather early in the public life of Jesus, when the streets were dark and the city was quiet, one of the leading citizens of Jerusalem knocked at the door of a young man who was fast becoming famous in Palestine as a rabbi, Jesus. Nicodemus was a Pharisee, which made him a very prominent figure in religious circles; he was also a ruler of the people, which probably means that he was the head of a very wealthy family and hence prominent in economic and social circles as well. At any rate we can safely assume that he was a man accustomed more to reverence and respect than to leg-pulling. At night there would be more opportunity for personal conversation and less opportunity for political disadvantage. Nicodemus was a good and pious man, but shrewd as a congressman in an election year.

Note how Nicodemus opened the conversation: "Rabbi, we know that thou hast come a teacher from God, for no one can work these signs that thou workest, unless God be with him." Addressing Jesus as Rabbi was a very clever bit—respectful and mildly flattering, like referring to a police sergeant as lieutenant. Jesus did not waste any time with preliminaries about His title or fancy compliments by way of exchange. Without any beating around the bush Jesus immediately made a statement about the kingdom of God that was utterly simple, absolutely fundamental, and astonishingly short. "Amen, amen, I say to thee, unless a man be born again, he cannot see the kingdom of God." 930132

The statement must have caught Nicodemus by surprise because his answer is completely lacking in the reverence and respectful docility with which he began the conversation. Instead there is blunt incredulity. "How can a man be born when he is old? Can he enter a second time into his mother's womb and be born again?" Nicodemus clearly was flustered. So with a great show of patience and the emphatic simplicity one uses when talking to a child Jesus explained Himself. "Amen, amen, I say to thee, unless a man be born again of water and the Spirit, he cannot enter into the kingdom of God." Obviously He was not talking biology, and to break it down into A, B, C's as one would with a child, Jesus added, "That which is born of the flesh is flesh; and that which is born of the Spirit is spirit."

With honest curiosity, but quite likely as an effort to recover his dignity with an intelligent sounding question, Nicodemus resumed his part of the conversation by saying, "How can these things be?" To that Jesus answered with a statement that must have been preceded by a chuckle, "Thou art a teacher in Israel and dost not know these things?"

It is not difficult to sympathize with Nicodemus' surprise at this talk of being born like a baby, at his age. Even his perplexity at Jesus' explanation is understandable; we would have been perplexed too. It is only in looking back through the years that we can see how Jesus, in the simple phrase, "born again of water and the Spirit," has captured the perfect explanation of Baptism.

Jesus said, "born again of the Spirit." Quite likely Nicodemus did not know who the Spirit was. In the Old Testament there are only vague allusions to the Trinity, and God did not expect that even great scholars would understand them.

It was not until much later in the public life of Jesus that He got around to talking about the Paraclete or the Holy Spirit. We know that the Spirit is the Third Person of the Trinity, the one whose mission it is to sanctify.

Then, too, Nicodemus knew of no precedent of a man being born of the Holy Spirit. Jesus was just becoming famous. Of course, He would be known as a Galilean; but it is not likely that anybody yet knew the facts about His conception and birth. Not knowing Mary, nobody could know about the Annunciation. Remember how the Angel Gabriel appeared to Mary and announced that she was to be the mother of the Messiah! She was perplexed about the details because, although she was betrothed, she had made a vow of virginity. Hence she answered, "How shall this happen, since I do not know man?" Then Gabriel explained to her how conception would occur leaving her vow and her virginity intact. "The Holy Spirit shall come upon thee and the power of the Most High shall overshadow thee; and therefore the Holy One to be born shall be called the Son of God." When Jesus said we were to be born again of the Spirit He was alluding to such a birth as His own. Nicodemus, however, could not know this at the time, but we are in a more favorable position. Because Jesus was born of the Holy Spirit, Gabriel said He would be called the Son of God. Because by Baptism we are born again of the Spirit, the catechism says that we are thereby made children of God.

Since the births are similar the effects are similar.

Jesus said "born again of water." Nicodemus must have been familiar with washing as a religious rite and with the Baptism of John the Baptist. The Pharisees had gone out to check up on John, and Nicodemus would either have been with them or heard their reports. Nevertheless, being born again of water did not make much sense to him. Again, we are in a better position to understand. Nicodemus did not know about the passion and death that Jesus was to suffer. That is where the difference lies. It is worthy of notice that even in this conversation Jesus did bring up the subject of His death just before their little talk concluded: "And as Moses lifted up the serpent in the desert, even so must the Son of Man be lifted up, that those who believe in Him may not perish, but may have life everlasting." All the sacraments apply to us the salvation brought about by the passion and death of Jesus. And when His side was opened with the lance, there came forth blood and water. Christian tradition has seen in the blood from the side of Christ the sacrament of the Eucharist, the sacred blood in the chalice at Mass; in the water from the side of Christ, the water in the sacrament of Baptism. We are cleansed from sin by His death. Hence, the being "born again of water" refers to the visible sign of the sacrament of Baptism, and to the reality it conveys.

In his Epistle to the Romans St. Paul wrote: "Do you not know that all we who have been baptized into Christ Jesus have been baptized into His death? For we were buried with Him by means of Baptism into death, in order that, just as Christ has arisen from the dead through the glory of the Father, so we also may walk in newness of life." The idea that Saint Paul had about Baptism being a kind of burial and rising again is not so clear in our present way of baptising by trickling a little water over the forehead. In ancient times Baptism was performed by immersing the whole body in water and then bringing it up again. Paul thus saw Baptism as being buried or put in the tomb as Christ was, and the rising from the waters as rising to a new life as Christ rose to the glorified life. It was a question of being born again, not of the womb but of the tomb. Knowing about the resurrection and having read St. Paul, we are in a much better position to understand the words of Jesus to Nicodemus.

Finally, it might be noted that in this explanation of Baptism, Jesus was using a biological analogy. Nicodemus' problem was in neglecting to look at it as an analogy. But even as an analogy we have a better grasp of the biological factors than Nicodemus could have had. Perhaps it is not always desirable to read modern theories into the analogies of Jesus but this is one time that the process is illuminating.

Modern biologists like to think of higher forms of life evolving from lower forms. The more poetic biologists picture little things creeping out of the watery chaos and climbing into trees and becoming birds or crawling about the landscape and becoming animals. And bit by bit the animals fit to survive do survive and get bigger and better until finally monkeys emerge to be followed by ourselves. Others even dream of ourselves evolving into yet grander creatures than we are. All in all, that is a good bit of poetry to take in one dose. But what is useful about this dream is this: the existence of a biological process that will lead to a higher type of life than human life as we know it. What is good about their dream is that it is true. What is bad about their dream is that they think this higher kind of life will occur without a cause or explanation, without Christ. But Jesus Himself uses biological terms and speaks of man as being born again to a more perfect kind of life.

Even without adding a dash of poetry to biology, this much is certainly true, that human life develops and evolves and grows. Babies are very small, built on a miniature scale, if you will; but they contain within themselves great capacity for growth and development both physically and mentally. As a matter of fact, the only way a baby can be kept from growing is by murdering it. Babies might differ by a few pounds or a few ounces but they are all babies. And when you talk about birth with reference to the human race, you talk about babies. In this analogy Jesus is pointing out that the life of grace follows the same picture. It starts out like human birth, small; but it contains within itself great power for growth and development.

In other words, Baptism introduces human nature to a new kind of life. On the one hand this new life is an improvement on the old, a step-up in the process of evolution. The life of grace not only obliterates sin, both personal and original, but adds something new. Taking away sin is like weeding out unhealthy strains that have crept into the race, as if, for example, left legs twisted into figure eight knots had become hereditary. Grace not only has this negative sort of effect, but positively adds a new life to the soul, new capacity for higher types of life function, like faith, hope and charity. But this new life is just a beginning. The grace of Baptism gives us only a wee, small share in the life of Christ. It is a seed of glory. And this seed of grace contains within itself great power for growth and development into the type of life that the risen Christ now lives with the Father in heaven, body and soul, glorious and immortal. Baptism gives us a new life, but it is the new life of a baby. It is not only a matter of culmination but also a matter of expectation.

From these speculative observations about the sacrament of Baptism, a number of practical conclusions follow. The sacraments are not just beautiful things to be looked at like a statue, but useful things to be put to work like a shovel.

The birth of a baby is a joyous event. Great preparations are made during the preceding months. Relatives and friends are informed by mother who begins to wear that pleased-with-herself look upon her face. Blankets, bottles, and booties pile up in the closet. As the time draws near father checks with the local cigar store, brothers and sisters, if any, speculate on the future balance of power in the battle between the sexes, and arrangements are made with aunt so-and-so to pinch-hit at the stove during mother's absence. And annually thereafter the event is commemorated with what is called a birthday party. All this is at it should be; the birth of a baby is a blessed event. A new son, a new daughter, a new brother, or a new sister is added to the family. Family life thereby promises to be just a little bit richer and fuller. It means one more hungry mouth to feed, but also one more cherubic face to kiss good-night; more socks to darn here and now, but more consolation in the twilight years.

The Baptism of a baby should be more joyous still. At least for a while the family has a saint in the house. A new member has been added to the mystical body of Christ. A new son, a new daughter, a new brother, or a new sister has been acquired who, by all the rules of the game, will be a companion in glory for all eternity. It would be a good thing if Baptisms were given at least as much importance as births. If birth announcements are worth the postage, why not Baptism announcements? If relatives and friends can find time during the week to visit the hospital, why could they not find time on a Sunday to attend the Baptism? Birthdays only mark a biological fact. If they are excuse enough for a celebration, why not the anniversary of Baptism? Without membership in the kingdom of heaven, membership in the human race is hardly worth the initiation fee.

It is only with the passage of years that one becomes familiar with the fact that babies are born in pain and travail. That one fact, however, has much to do with the deep feelings of love between mother and child. When one appreciates the price, one begins to appreciate the product a little more. Our life is a gift that has been dearly paid for with suffering. So, too, in being born again of water and the Spirit, the price for the gift of this new life has been pain and travail, passion and death. If for no other reason, the price itself should lead one to appreciate the life of grace just a little bit more.

Usually when babies are born they weigh between six and eight pounds. At first they lose a bit of weight, which throws mother into a panic if she has not been briefed on the phenomenon before hand. Thereafter, however, life is mostly a pattern of adding pounds. There is a steady increase up until about the twenties after which things level off until about the forties, at which date the numbers on the scale enlarge relentlessly. To live is to grow. If it should happen by some miscarriage of nature that junior weighed only six pounds at the ripe old age of ten, parents would be unspeakably alarmed, neighbors would be astounded, and medical science would be mystified in three different languages. Certainly junior would end up in a bottle in a medical museum. The law of life is a law of growth. Grace is a new kind of life, and it, too, has a law of growth. Baptism is birth to this new kind of life. The Christian who is born again of water and the Spirit and fails to grow is ten times more a freak than the above mentioned junior. What is really remarkable is that he can pass for normal among the members of the kingdom of God.

growing up

The catechism tells us that Confirmation is a sacrament that makes us strong and perfect Christians and soldiers of Jesus Christ. It, too, is a very nice sort of service for the church to have. It is an appeal to youth, or at least to what there is of youthfulness in men, and everybody agrees that the youths are important in any man's country. Of course, their assistance is not too welcome on the policy level, but everyone knows that in the battles of any one generation, it will be up to the youth of the land to shoulder the burden, shed the blood, and shape the future.

As a matter of fact, just about every kind of society has some sort of ceremony welcoming boys and girls into the august ranks of men and women. Of course, growing up is an inevitable sort of process that society cannot do anything about anyway. But generally speaking, societies, whether they be the tribe or the Knights of Columbus, try to take advantage of the process. In tribal life when a boy kills his first deer with a bow and arrow made with his own hands, there will be some sort of ceremony which gives public recognition to him as a man. Since he is going to be killing deer anyway, it is well to have him on the side of society where his efforts will not be a boyhood adventure but a responsible social achievement beneficial to the food supply of the tribe. Societies, from the Nazis to the Knights of Columbus, from the Boy Scouts to the bush leagues, all have ceremonies and uniforms and programs which appeal to youth, which commemorate the fact that boys and girls are growing up, which try to win their vitality and strength and enthusiasm and skill to the side of this or that adult group.

Confirmation is an appeal to youth. It commemorates the fact that a Christian is no longer an infant. It makes an adult Christian of him, a soldier of Jesus Christ. Without doubt, Confirmation is a very nice sort of service for the Church to have. But Jesus did not invent sacraments just because they were nice to have. He did not invent Confirmation just to give the pastor an excuse for insisting on a refresher course in catechism before the children left his school. Jesus invented each and every sacrament because He knew each and every sacrament was needed. In other words, Jesus instituted Confirmation, not because it was nice, but because it was necessary.

Jesus must have had some special motive which led Him to produce this masterpiece. He must have had some special insight into the life of grace and the nature of man which led Him to institute this sacrament. One might put the question of the necessity of having Confirmation more pointedly by asking why Jesus instituted two sacraments, Baptism and Confirmation, when He could have had one sacrament do both jobs.

Remember that in the sacraments Jesus is speaking to us. He is teaching us something about the life of grace, appealing to some deep need in our nature. A good teacher teaches just one lesson at a time lest the students get all mixed up. A good psychologist appeals to only one impulse, one psychic requirement at a time, lest he move the subject like a pin wheel instead of like an arrow.

Now there are many special effects of grace, many phases in the life of grace, just as there are many phases in natural human life. Jesus has arranged that there be a special sacrament to deal with each of these special effects of grace. Thus, He invented Baptism as a reminder that we needed to be saved from original sin and to teach us that in that moment we were born again to a new and special kind of life, a life which comes from the Spirit of God. So too He invented a second sacrament to teach us that it is the same Spirit by whom we are strengthened, to teach us that the Spirit not only gives life in the first place but also brings it to maturity.

Actually there are three sacraments which strengthen us: Confirmation, the Eucharist, and Extreme Unction, but they all strengthen us in a different way and with a different kind of strength. After all, it takes one kind of strength to swing a pick in a coal mine and another kind of strength to jump out of bed for early Mass on Sunday; many husky characters sleep late on Sunday. Extreme Unction gives one the strength to face death with tranquillity. The Eucharist gives one the strength to love God above all other lovable things in the whole world. But Confirmation strengthens one in a different way; it strengthens one for what there is of battle and struggle and contest in adult Christian life.

Thus, just as we were not born of our mothers in grace to show us that this life is a special gift from God, so, too, we are not automatically strengthened in grace, made strong by the Spirit of God for what there is of struggle in the Christian life. Without the reminder of Baptism, men would forget their need for a Savior. Without Confirmation, one of two things would happen: either one would try to struggle all alone or one would not struggle at all. As a matter of fact, we would probably try struggling by ourselves and end up by throwing in the sponge. In a fight against overwhelming odds, fighting alone is not fun in any man's language. In settling a difference of opinion behind the barn, a young man might feel fully competent to hold up his end of the disagreement;

but facing the pressure of a pagan environment is another matter. Without the Spirit of God to strengthen us in that battle, every man would be sadly handicapped. This seems to be the basic reason why Jesus arranged things so that this special grace should come to us through a special visible sign.

Up to this point, the argument for the necessity of Confirmation has been based almost completely on the idea that the sacraments teach us a lesson about the life of grace. But remember that the sacraments are also masterpieces of art. They appeal to more than the mind and the memory; they appeal to deep-seated human feelings and needs. The necessity of Confirmation becomes clearer, perhaps, when the sacrament is looked upon as a product of Christ's artistry. What art is involved here? It would seem to be the art of encouraging. After all, the special kind of strengthening that a man needs before a battle and in a struggle is courage. And encouragement, like reminding, is a very special kind of art. Suppose a fighter is being prepared for the ring. His seconds hover around him. Listlessly swinging a towel, wearing foot-long faces and moaning about the size of the opponent is hardly calculated to boost the morale of their champion, especially if word gets about that they have put a few odd dollars on the other fighter. Really good seconds massage their champion's muscles to build up muscle tone, pound him on the back, and say encouraging things to him. They tell him how he can slaughter that other fighter with one hand tied behind his back, that the bigger they come the harder they fall. The words and the gestures make a good deal of difference. The same thing is true with soldiers preparing for battle. Ragged, nondescript uniforms, groans about the inadequacy and the futility of it all, and funereal dirges are a prelude to defeat. Fighting men need snappy uniforms, first-rate equipment, and an enthusiastic conviction about the nobility of their cause. In any kind of a fight, morale is important, and morale building is a fine art if ever there was one.

The kind of strength that strong and perfect Christians and soldiers of Jesus Christ need is courage. Confirmation is designed to give them just that. It is a masterpiece in the art of morale building, of encouraging. This is evident both in the signs employed in giving the sacrament and in the special way in which this sacrament was instituted.

Confirmation has about it the air of athletic preparation. There is the anointing with oil, the blow upon the cheek. It has about it, too, an air of military preparation. The anointing is done in the sign of the cross which is the Christian's badge of office just as the flag under which he fights is a special banner to the soldier. Most of these ceremonies have been introduced into the sacrament of Confirmation by the Church who thereby has interpreted and applied the mind of Christ.

This point, that Confirmation is a masterpiece in the art of encouragement, is also evident in the way it was instituted. Nobody can encourage a fighter like a champion. Nobody can encourage a soldier like a victorious soldier, a veteran of the wars. Hence, when Jesus came to institute the sacrament of Confirmation He did not do it by assigning the matter to be used and the words to be spoken. He left it the Church to decide that. He instituted Confirmation by promising to send the Holy Spirit who was actually going to strengthen us, working in and through the matter and the words. However, the Holy Spirit was not sent until after Jesus had suffered and died, until after He was the victorious soldier, a battle-scarred veteran of the same war we fight.

Thus John writes, "For the spirit had not yet been given, since Jesus had not yet been glorified" (7:39). And again Jesus said, "It is expedient for you that I depart. For if I do not go, the Advocate will not come to you; but if I go, I will send him to you" (John 16:7). Thus the institution of the sacrament was entirely unique. He instituted Baptism by being baptized and by instructing the Apostles to go and baptize all nations. He instituted the Eucharist, not during the sermon on the Bread of Life wherein He promised it, but at the Last Supper when He consecrated bread and wine and gave it to them to eat. He instituted the sacrament of Orders by telling them to do this in commemoration of Him. He instituted the sacrament of Penance by giving the Apostles the power to forgive sins. But the sacrament of Confirmation He instituted by promising something. The actual strengthening that it was to give did not occur until after He had suffered, died, and ascended into heaven as He had promised. It was a promise that was to be fulfilled only by a champion crowned with victory.

In other words, the fullness of grace which is received in Confirmation is the work of the Holy Spirit who is sent to us by the glorified Christ. Just as the fullness of grace was sent to the Apostles on Pentecost, so too this fullness comes to us in Confirmation. Confirmation is our Pentecost. Just as Pentecost made all the difference in the world in the Apostles' morale, so too this sacrament should make us strong and courageous like them, once they had received the fullness of the Spirit. When Jesus promised to send the Holy Spirit, the Advocate, only after He had suffered and was glorified, and on the condition that He had suffered and was glorified, He instituted the sacrament of Confirmation. This special grace came the first time in a very special manner at Pentecost—in tongues of fire. But the same grace comes in what we now call the Sacrament of Confirmation.

In the early days of the Church, Confirmation was given right after Baptism, which meant, frequently enough, that it was given to infants. Frequently enough in our times, when a man is converted late in life or comes to die and has not been confirmed, Confirmation is administered to the senile. But these occasional differences in the age of the one receiving Confirmation should not obscure the basic point of the sacrament. After all, the general practice of the Church now is that one receives the sacrament at about fourteen, at that time in life we describe as youth, the time at which childhood ceases and mature adult life begins. Confirmation is an appeal to youth, or at least to what is youthful in the human heart.

At about fourteen, the adolescent is beginning to try his first few experimental steps toward maturity. The little girl begins to want to dress and act like the lady. The little boy wants long pants; he wants to swagger and show off his muscles. In the adolescent years nature is yearning for maturity. However, at the same time there is always a feeling of insufficiency. For example, boys go around in gangs because each one is just a little bit timid about swaggering alone. In other words, at that time in life, what the youth needs is not only to be treated and accepted as an adult, but also to be unobtrusively supported with encouragement.

The societies alluded to at the beginning of the chapter all introduce the youth to activities beyond the family circle, activities that belong to adult life. They accept him as an adult. At the same time, however, they support him with the encouragement of the group. In a way Confirmation has a similar function in the life of grace. It accepts the budding Christian as adult and mature in the Christian life, as capable of the behavior appropriate to maturity. But on the other hand it gives strength and support and encouragement to allay any feelings of insufficiency.

Now it is quite true that Confirmation time provides an excellent opportunity to insist upon a refresher course in catechism. But, if the true import of Confirmation is to be fulfilled, this should be a special type of instruction. If Confirmation is to produce a mature and perfect Christian, the instruction should be on a more mature and adult level. Simple repetition of the same memorized lessons which were insisted on at the age of seven will not be adequate. Instruction must be imparted on a mature level before those to be confirmed will begin to think on a mature level. And if the practice of the Church is to confirm youths at about fourteen, it is not likely that the Church has miscalculated on the psychological capacities of the young men and women involved.

Again, it would be well if Confirmation marked a change not only in the type of instruction imparted but in the discipline as well. Childhood is best provided for with protection. In as much as it is possible, Christian children should be sheltered from the influences of the pagan world in which we live. But it is possible to give too much shelter. If Christians are going to live in the world as it actually exists, they are going to have to meet it in terms of battle. And it would seem that Confirmation might well mark the turning point at which protection is withdrawn and a military sort of enterprise is initiated. Unless there is an appropriate readjustment in instruction and discipline parallel to the spiritual reality of the sacrament of Confirmation, the real import of this great experience is likely to be lost.

Confirmation is a masterpiece in the art of encouraging. It is an appeal to youth. It is the sacrament of growing up. And the sooner those who are confirmed can get the idea into their heads that they are supposed to be grown-up Christians, the more likely it is that they will act that way. Otherwise it is like insisting that a boy is old enough to work for the tribe killing deer, but not old enough to play with bows and arrows.

full of spirit

Theologians can often be side-tracked by intriguing problems of an erudite nature. If you were to ask a theologian what he thought about Confirmation, likely as not he would light on the question of who established the matter and form of the sacrament—i.e., who invented the actual details of the sacrament. Now it is true that only Jesus can institute a sacrament. The Church can not. But the Church can arrange and has arranged and rearranged many of the details of the sacraments. And the beautiful job the Church has done in arranging the details of the sacrament of Confirmation is much more interesting than the extent of her authority in this matter. What the picture means is more interesting than who held the paint pot.

It can happen that Confirmation will be administered by the pastor. For example, if the bishop is unavailable and one of the pastor's flock is sick unto death, the pastor can confirm him. Likely as not the scene would be a sick-room and Father would be prosaically garmented in his black suit, and none too handsomely at that, having been put on in a hurry in the middle of the night. This is a possible picture, but it is not the typical picture of Confirmation. All of the essential elements of Confirmation are present, but they do not stand out so clearly as in the typical picture which includes a bishop, a church, and boys and girls.

Except for a bit of purple under his collar, and perhaps a flash of gold chain across his vest, a bishop looks a good deal like a priest when he walks down the street. True, they do run a bit more to dignity and frequently wear a longer coat, but nevertheless they are usually relatively inconspicuous on the street. Not so at Confirmation. No matter how small the bishop may be, the mitre gives him height, the cope adds splendor, and the crozier gives him the unmistakable majesty of pastoral authority. In the Church, the bishop is a very important man. He is a successor to the Apostles, and at Confirmation he appears in all his dignity. Splendidly arrayed in cope and mitre, his crozier in his hand, he solemnly passes along the communion rail, tracing a cross in oil on the forehead of each person to be confirmed. While he does it he says: "I consign thee with the sign of the cross and confirm thee with the chrism of salvation. In the name of the Father, and of the Son and of the

Holy Ghost. Amen." Then he reaches back with his hand and gives each a slight blow on the cheek. Such is the typical picture of Confirmation.

In this ceremony the Church has contrived to give concrete form to the sacrament which Christ promised as the fullness of the Holy Spirit. Christ meant this sacrament to be a gesture of encouragement, and from this point of view all the little details which the Church has arranged make good sense.

In the first place, consider the matter which the bishop uses, chrism which is a mixture of olive oil with a small portion of balsam. This anointing is supposed to have about it the obvious note of athletic preparation. In ancient times when these details were worked out, athletes would be massaged with something like this rather than rubbing alcohol or witch-hazel or wintergreen. After all, rubbing alcohol is a modern invention.

But the oil has a deeper significance too. It signifies the fullness of the Holy Spirit which comes through the sacrament. Nowadays we use oil to lubricate machinery or in the construction of a salad. But the significance of the oil in the sacrament of Confirmation lies buried in the Old Testament, for example in the Forty-fourth Psalm where it is prophecied of the Messias that "he will be anointed with oil of gladness," meaning by that the fullness of the Holy Spirit. As a matter of fact, this is why Jesus is called "Christ." "Christ" is not a last name like "Smith" or "Jones." It means "The

Anointed One," and He was called that because the Holy Spirit was with Him. Being anointed with the oil of gladness was a figure of speech referring to this fullness of the Holy Spirit. That is why anointing with oil is the matter for the sacrament of Confirmation in which the fullness of the Spirit is given to us.

Not any old kind of oil is used; only olive oil. An obvious reason for this is that olive oil is one of the finest kinds of oil; it is oil *par excellence*. It is true that in the United States olive oil is not used very much, except perhaps in California. But when an Italian says "oil" he means olive oil. Really, only the finest kind of oil can signify the Holy Spirit. This is one of the reasons St. Thomas alleges for using olive oil, and St. Thomas was an Italian. He adds another reason, though: He notes that olive trees stay green all year around. They are one of the few trees that have leaves instead of needles that do stay green all the time. This helps to signify the vitality and fullness of life that comes through the Holy Spirit.

Chrism is a mixture of olive oil and balsam. Now, balsam is a sweet smelling resin that comes from certain trees. It mixes rather well with oil and gives it a perfumed odor. Vegetable oils generally have a tendency to turn rancid with age; the balsam prevents that. But it also signifies that the fullness of the Holy Spirit which is given in this sacrament is to be communicated to others like a sweet odor. We always say in moments when Junior speaks out of turn that little children are to be seen and not heard. The idea is that communication belongs to adults. Confirmation makes a child an adult as far as the Spirit is concerned. By this sacrament the sweetness of the Holy Spirit is supposed to be communicated as becomes an adult Christian.

Jesus instituted the sacrament of Confirmation by promising to send the fullness of the Spirit. This promise was fulfilled for the Apostles and disciples at Pentecost. It is fulfilled for the rest of us in Confirmation. The details of Confirmation have been worked out so that the matter of the sacrament parallels the events at Pentecost. At Pentecost the visible sign was tongues of fire. The Apostles and disciples and Mary the mother of Jesus were assembled in the Upper Room praying. There was a sound like a great wind and tongues of fire hovered over the head of each. The oil in confirmation is just oil; it is oil in the passive and inert state. The tongues of fire at Pentecost referred to oil in the active state of giving off heat and light. After all, the Apostles and disciples received the Holy Spirit in a more active way than we do in Confirmation. They were the founding fathers of the Church. They were no longer just simple lay people. Note, too, that the fire came in the shape of tongues. The visible sign at Pentecost also gets across the same idea as the balsam in chrism. Both the use of the tongue and a sweet odor have to do with communication. The communication which the fullness of the Spirit brought to the Apostles at Pentecost was an active preaching of the word of God; in Confirmation it is more a question of the sweet odor of example.

Consider the words which the Bishop uses. "I consign thee with the sign of the cross and I confirm thee with the chrism of salvation. In the name of the Father and of the Son and of the Holy Ghost. Amen." "I consign thee with the sign of the cross" means that one is being given the insignia or badge of his new role as a soldier of Jesus Christ. From the time of Constantine the sign of the Christian has been the sign of the cross. Whether against the Moslems in the middle ages or against the Communists in the twentieth century, Christians wage war under the banner of the cross. What the crescent is to the Mohammedan and the hammer and sickle to the Communist, the cross is to the Christian. The words, "I confirm thee with the chrism of salvation," indicate the strengthening by the Holy Spirit which is occurring. These words explain the mute sign of the anointing so that there will be no mistake about what the anointing with chrism means. "In the name of the Father and of the Son and of the Holy Ghost" indicate the ultimate source of this strength. The mission of the Holy Ghost is from the bosom of the Triune God.

The anointing is done on the forehead, and not just because the forehead is the handiest place as the bishop passes down the rail. When you are preparing a boxer for the ring you massage and flex his arms, especially the old biceps. When you are preparing a runner for the course you massage and flex his leg muscles. In the ring the contest is a matter of punch and in the stadium the contest is a matter of sprint. The anointing in Confirmation follows the same pattern and the battle envisaged is one involving the head. Confirmation strengthens us in a very special kind of fight—the confession of the faith. One might well argue the point that, if confessing the faith is the contest involved, it might have been better to oil up the tongue. Saint Thomas thought of that same point by way of objection. His answer is a classic. Apparently, like the rest of us, he had been bored by a good bit of witless speech in his time, perhaps some of it purportedly a defense or confession of the Christian faith. At any rate, he answers the objection by noting that speech is meaningless unless it proceeds from the mind, and to indicate that the confession of the faith should be both free and intelligent the forehead is anointed instead of the tongue.

Then, too, remember that this anointing is a matter of consigning with the sign of the cross, of giving a soldier his insignia of office. Soldiers generally wear their insignia in a fairly prominent place, either on their cap, their lapels, or epaulets; so in Confirmation the most prominent part of the body is singled out—the forehead. Generally when you look at a man you look at his eyes. If you look at his mouth he begins to wonder if his teeth are clean. And when you look at the eyes you look at the forehead. That makes the forehead the ideal spot for consigning with the sign of the cross.

Not only are the face and forehead the most prominent portion of a man, but it is in the face especially that fear and shame become evident. Fear makes the face turn white and shame makes it turn red. It is fear and shame that interfere with the public profession of faith. Confirmation strengthens us against these things. Hence it is most appropriate that the anointing be done in the place where fear and shame show on a person.

One last idea about anointing the forehead in Confirmation: It indicates a development and growth in the grace that has been given in Baptism. Unfortunately the whole idea of using oil on the body is almost unknown in our days. At best a little pomade is used to keep the hair slick, or some cold cream is used by the ladies to keep their skin lovely. But in ancient times, especially in the climate of Palestine, oil was used rather profusely as a hair and skin dressing, as the hot, dry air would remove much of the natural oil. Thus, for example, one of the basic courtesies shown a guest would be to pour some scented oil upon his head, in much the same spirit as we offer a newly arrived traveler a cup of coffee or some other restorative. In Baptism the crown of the head is anointed; in Confirmation the forehead, to indicate the gradual progress of the life of grace in absorbing our

full of spirit **63**

whole personality. Grace, as it were, first gives faith and then through faith integrates and perfects the rest of human nature.

Finally, it is the bishop who ordinarily gives this sacrament. Confirmation is a sacrament which makes us perfect Christians and soldiers. A bishop is the most appropriate minister for such a sacrament. Basically it is the priest who baptizes and brings people into the Church. But it is the bishop who is supposed to bring the flock to the state of Christian perfection. Furthermore, it is the general of the army who comes around to deliver the final orders to the troops before they enter into battle. In the recent unpleasantness with Hitler, General Patton became famous for his speeches to the troops in such circumstances. A bishop is an important figure in the Church, and is like a general in the army. Hence it is most appropriate that he come around and administer Confirmation to the children of the parish. For it is Confirmation that makes them soldiers of Jesus Christ and starts them off into the battle of the Christian life. As a matter of fact, in our times a bishop's life is rather taken up with administrative affairs. He does not have the time to visit the parishes very often. But busy as he is, he still comes around for Confirmation. Nobody else can do the job of inspiring enthusiasm in the troops quite like a bishop.

At the end of the ceremony the bishop gives each a slight blow on the cheek. Usually the children have been coached for this and keep one eye on the bishop's right hand. It is the one part of the whole affair calculated to impress. This blow is supposed to have about it the spirit of "get in there and fight like a man now." It has something of the spirit of cuffing a ball player on the back to give him encouragement. Then, too, this blow is reminiscent of the blow on the head that Jesus suffered from the hands of the soldiers who mocked Him before the crucifixion. In the free and intelligent profession of the faith, the type of blow that the Christian shall suffer will be mockery. The world buffets with its scorn. In Confirmation this blow is not only a bit of encouragement; it is also a foretaste of what is to come.

Basically, this is the meaning of the sacrament of Confirmation. This is what the visible signs are trying to say. What with new suits and worry about the bishop's firm right hand, one is likely to see the picture in a blurred sort of way. It is a good idea to attend Confirmation in the parish church each year and witness the ceremony over and over. Never can one see this picture too often. Furthermore, it should be a public affair with all the parishioners present. Inducting soldiers in the army of Jesus Christ is not a private party for the bishop or a personal experience for those confirmed. It is a public social action. A soldier is everybody's business. He is fighting everybody's fight. The battle of the faith is never like settling a difference of opinion behind the barn. It is a social act, an act of the Mystical Body of Christ.

chapter seven

courageous christians

If you walk into an art gallery with the hope of acquiring a deeper appreciation of the pictures and statues, or if you walk into a shop where such things are sold, the guide or the clerk will begin to tell you about what the pictures mean or about the circumstances which led the artist to paint them. If he does not tell you, you will probably ask him. But usually guides in art galleries and salesmen in art stores do not need to be asked; they positively effervesce with information of this sort, and it is extremely difficult for the unwashed admirer to get a question in edge-wise. Art salesmen are as difficult to converse with on a blow-by-blow basis as ardent barbers. Explanations of meaning, of interpretation, of technique, and of history just naturally go with works of art. In the same way it is important to give these kinds of explanations about the sacraments. And for the last two chapters that is just what we have been doing about Confirmation.

However, the sacraments are not just to be looked at like a picture, or listened to like a symphony. Theologians say that the sacraments are practical signs. They mean practical like an automobile or a wheel-barrow is practical. When you walk into an automobile dealer's show-room you do not ask what the latest model means or what circumstances led the manufacturer to build it. You ask practical questions like how fast the new model will travel, how powerful the motor is, how many miles this internal combustion machine will travel on a gallon of gasoline. If the salesman evades these questions, you leave the place muttering under your breath in perplexity and look for another dealer. But auto salesmen are usually overwhelming in praise of the practical advantages of their product and it is more likely that you will depart poor than perplexed. It is likewise important to answer questions of a practical nature about the sacraments. It is important to know exactly just how powerful Confirmation is, just what it will do for a Christian.

This chapter is going to be about Confirmation from the practical point of view. We will consider what this sacrament is supposed to do for us, and what are its effects. Theologians say there are two effects which come from Confirmation: the character of Confirmation, and the grace of Confirmation.

Most likely it is because the point itself is obscure, but theologians are not too expansive and illuminating when they get around to explaining the character of Confirmation. Some points, however, are clear. In the first place, this character is something new and real added to the soul. It is something just as real as the shape of a key hole which makes it possible for the door to be unlocked by the key. But the character which comes as an effect of Confirmation is spiritual like grace. It does not make the soul good the way grace does. Grace is something new and real added to the soul and it actually sanctifies us; the character does not. A man can have the baptismal character, the character that comes with Confirmation, or the priestly character and still have a soul black as pitch and most displeasing in the sight of God. As a matter of fact, it is not at all inconceivable that there are quite a few of these characters in hell. Which is a thing that cannot be said for a soul sanctified by grace.

Make no mistake. This character is none the less a very useful thing to have. Its usefulness parallels the usefulness of the baptismal character. The baptismal character makes it possible for a man to receive the other sacraments. If a man has not been baptized with water he does not have this character. If he should tell his sins to the priest and the priest should say the words of absolution, no sacrament of Penance would occur. If he should be ordained by a bishop, the man would still not be a priest. The baptismal character makes it possible for us to receive the other sacraments, and without it they cannot really be received. The character of Confirmation makes it possible for us to receive the other sacraments, and especially the Eucharist, in a more abundant way, in a way that makes these sacraments more efficacious in working on our souls. To borrow a metaphor from the sport of kings, it moves the odds in our favor.

Then, too, this character is like a check book with reference to the grace of Confirmation. If you have a check book and a bank book, you have a right to the money in the bank and can convert it into merchandise and the necessities and luxuries of life whenever you want. The confirmational character gives us a right to the graces that a strong and perfect Christian needs, the graces that a soldier of Jesus Christ requires in the battle of life. As a matter of fact, the medieval theologians went so far as to say that these graces came to us through this character. And by that word "through" they meant "through an instrument," as, for example, the letter comes from the ardent scribe "through" the ball-point pen, unromantic as it may sound. Maybe the theologians are a little sketchy in speaking about the confirmational character, but that is more because the subject is mysterious than because it is unreal. They thought about the character of Confirmation as something very real and very important. It was not something unreal like a man assuming a character in a play, like the local butcher playing Rip Van Winkle which involves little more than gluing whiskers on the chin. The Confirmational character changes the soul. The soul of the butcher remains unsullied by the addition of whiskers to his chin, and a bit of the Bronx cheer from the audience is sure to cure him of dramatic enthusiasm. But the Christian soul can never get over being a soldier of Jesus Christ.

There have been vague allusions made to the special grace or set of graces which come to the soul from Confirmation. Perhaps it will help to get across the idea of what this grace is if the question of when it comes is considered first. In some sacraments the grace comes right away, while the water is being poured or the words are being said. But some sacraments have a sort of delayed action. When you are baptized you then and there receive the baptismal grace. When you go to confession, right then and there your sins are taken away. They are gone by the time the priest has finished pronouncing the formula of absolution. You walk out of the box innocent as a baby and have a right to feel that way; there is no question of having the feeling of relief hit you three days later while shaving. But when you are married or ordained a priest, it does not necessarily mean that you get the special graces of these sacraments right then and there in the sanctuary. It can happen that you walk out of the church happier but no holier than when you walked in. The grace of the sacrament of Matrimony gives the strength to be a good Christian parent day by day as the duties of parenthood require—when the son and heir cries in the middle of the night, when junior announces his first date. The grace of the sacrament of Orders is supposed to enable the priest to do holy things in a holy way. The priest gets these graces day by day as needed, when he says Mass for the Sisters at six in the morning, at ten minutes after nine on Saturday evening when the stragglers come for confession, at two o'clock in the night when the telephone rings about a sick call. Confirmation works like this, too. The grace comes, not right in Church while the bishop is consigning us with the sign of the cross, but out in the market place years later, or wherever a man fights the good fight as a soldier of Jesus Christ.

Enough hints have been dropped by now to make it pretty obvious what the grace of Confirmation actually does. In a nut shell, this grace gives fortitude, or to use a more familiar term, courage. After all, Confirmation is a masterpiece in the art of encouragement. The whole point of this grace is to strengthen us for battle, and the kind of strengthening that soldiers need in the face of combat is obviously courage.

This grace of Confirmation fortifies the spirit for battle but not just any old kind of battle. It gives no promise of success on the football field, unless, of course, you happen to play for Notre Dame.

Confirmation encourages one for a more distinctly Christian kind of battle. Now, there are many different kinds of Christian battles: the battle one has to wage with self to keep from cheating with the candy bars during Lent, for example. But Confirmation is little help during Lent. The battle for which Confirmation strengthens us is a very special kind of battle, the battle involved in giving public testimony to the faith. Centuries ago Jesus must have envisaged that Christians would always be living in an unkind and pagan world that would be more or less hostile to the faith. After all it does not take any special sturdiness of soul to publicly admit to being a Christian and to actually live publicly as a Christian in an environment where everybody is a good Christian. Jesus knew that the world was never going to be one great big cloister filled to overflowing with seraphic faces and pious sighs. He met a good deal of opposition in His brief public life and He knew that we would, too, right up to the bitter end.

The dimensions that this battle takes on and the type of hostility that the Christian meets in the profession of his faith vary from age to age. For some ages, being a Christian involved nourishing the lions. In other ages it involved bashing in a Turk's head with a battle ax before he upset the circulatory system with his scimitar. Now it might involve having to be content with a second-rate job because one does not wear a pin with a scimitar on it. Hence it is that through the ages there has been a certain amount of variety in the way that Christians have understood this special grace of Confirmation.

For example, in the early church Confirmation was looked upon as giving one the courage to go through with martyrdom when called upon. By the character of Confirmation one was set aside as an official of the church, whose office it was to give public testimony to the Faith by suffering death in a Roman arena. In those days martyrdom was connected with the public testimony to the Faith in a very special way. It was a time when the church was underground. There were no big public churches, no great processions through the streets, no priests' names in the telephone directory, no signs in the hotels announcing the times of Masses at the near-by Church, no Eucharistic Congresses, and no pictures of bishops in the newspapers. But the one time that the Church and the Faith of Jesus Christ did become public and visible, and in a very unmistakable fashion, was at a martyrdom, when a Christian was up for execution for being a Christian. They could usually escape the inconvenience of martyrdom by offering incense to the pagan gods. But refusal meant ending up as lion food at big public games in a Roman stadium. Hence, their courage in facing such a death was directly and unmistakably connected with the public testimony of faith in Jesus Christ. It was the one big chance to advertise the

Faith in a very hostile environment, and it was not easy.

In recent times Pope Pius XI has called Confirmation the sacrament of Catholic Action. Catholic Action is basically the cell technique of the Marxists applied to the task of changing our pagan environment to Christian living. These cells are small combat teams organized on natural social levels—factory workers, students, white collar workers, etc. They first bring into sharp focus the factors in each environment that militate against living a Christian life. Then they plan and carry into effect projects which will change that environment from being positively bad to being positively good. Naturally this sort of thing takes a lot of prudence, but it also takes a lot of courage, the kind of courage that is required in the public testimony of the Faith. No communist likes to be beaten at his own game.

Pope Pius XI did much to bring our understanding of the grace of Confirmation up to date. Since then quite a few books have been written about Confirmation as the sacrament of Catholic Action. This is a very fine thing. But actually very few American Catholics are members of a Catholic Action cell . . . which is not a very fine thing. But it is the way things are at the present time. This does not mean, however, that the ordinary American Catholic is not called upon in his own environment to give public testimony to the Faith, and to give it in a way that makes special demands upon one's courage.

But when it comes to the public testimony of the Faith for just the ordinary Catholic in just ordinary circumstances, a few points should be kept in mind. In the first place, the flashing of sodality buttons in lapels, the rattle of rosaries, and ecstatic accounts of novenas and miracles are of little value in publicizing the Faith of Jesus Christ. For the most part, people outside the Church are not too benevolently disposed toward the man-made aspects of the Catholic Church. The public testimony of the Faith has to be on more essential points of Christianity, more genuinely a Christian article. The beatitudes would be a good starting place. In an age when greed is the rage and possessions are the badge of distinction, it takes courage to live publicly "poor in spirit." But the Christian who has the courage of his convictions and actually lives up to this beatitude will give as big a jolt to his environment as any martyr in a Roman arena. And among men who look upon it as especially manly to get together and exchange dirty stories, it takes courage to be "clean of heart" and dissociate oneself from the spirit of the group. But this is the kind of public profession of faith that lies within the daily possibilities of every Catholic. And Confirmation gives one the grace to do it without fear or shame.

Again, much of the growth of the Church in this country has been the work of immigrants. Only bit by bit has the Church in America been able to establish itself publicly as a non-foreign element in our country's life. But being a minority group and being frequently misunderstood, we have developed the inferiority complex that such groups so frequently have. As a group we defend with fanatic zeal any real or fancied encroachment upon our rights. We make speeches, write editorials, and telegraph congressmen about a few paltry textbooks that do not make much difference one way or another. And in our fanatic zeal we lose friends that we can hardly do without when larger and more clear-cut issues come up. At the other extreme, as individual Catholics we make too great an effort to be compliant. For example, if Protestant friends are going to be in the house for the evening meal, the family rosary goes by the board lest the visitors in the house be offended.

Finally, the best advertisement is a satisfied customer. The Christian way of life has never been the most comfortable way of life. It has always demanded a certain amount of heroic virtue in every age. And the man who has the courage to live that way of life joyfully in twentieth-century America is the man who is going to bring America to Christ.

chapter eight

sinners delight

Like all the other sacraments, Penance is a masterpiece of Christ's artistic genius, a thing of beauty. For the purpose of demonstrating this point, it might prove useful to consider Penance as a masterpiece in the art of healing. Now, a doctor does not say to himself in the morning, "I'll give my first six patients aspirin and the second six liver pills." He suits the medicine to the disease. After all, his first patient of the morning might be suffering from a hang-nail. So, too, Christ has suited this sacrament to the psychological needs of the contrite sinner. Sometimes we get to thinking that psychology is a twentieth-century invention, when for the most part all that has been invented is the big words. For untold centuries there have been geniuses who have understood the workings of the human psyche, and first and foremost among these was Our Lord.

A few case histories should suffice to establish the point that Jesus understood the psychological requirements of guilt feelings. The fact that both of them involve women is in no way a reflection on the fair sex but only helps to prove the point. The first case has to do with a woman usually named Mary Magdalene but identified by St. Luke only as a woman who was a sinner in the city. All we know about her before she wept at the feet of Jesus is that she was famous enough in her line of work so that the Pharisee who was Jesus' host knew all about her, that she was opulent enough to have an alabaster jar of ointment, and that she was feminine through and through. By some importunity she gained entrance to the dining room of a private residence where Jesus was reclining at table. Most likely they were eating in the prevalent Hebrew fashion: propped on one elbow on a low couch with feet extended away from the table. Apparently the woman had enough pluck to brazen her way into the room, but it is rather difficult to conjecture what she had in mind to do. Quite likely she had not thought things out too far, for what she actually did could hardly have been thought out. Standing behind Him, she impulsively stooped and kissed His feet. Then, unexpectedly, she broke into tears and in her confusion tried to dry the wet feet with the handiest thing she had, her long hair. In the silence that ensued, Jesus defended her with the parable of the money lender who had two debtors, and also by rebuking His host for having neglected the ordinary courtesies which this woman had so touchingly provided. Then He forgave her sins. Every detail in this episode shows that Jesus is in complete command of the situation, the perfect gentleman, and profoundly sympathetic. Embarrased by the sudden emotional break as she was, Jesus commended it as social grace. She was a famous sinner and an unwelcome intruder in a Pharisee's house. Jesus compared her to the Pharisee and the latter came off second best. But most of all, Jesus welcomed her attention and showed a deep appreciation of the motive which prompted it: love.

The other case involves a woman who was apprehended in adultery and who was actually at the mercy of the Scribes and Pharisees when she was brought to Jesus. They, of course, were going to stone her in accordance with the Mosaic Law. Being apprehended in adultery must have been a severe blow to her composure, and the prospect of death at the hands of self-righteous fanatics was hardly calculated to soothe the spirit. With all the crowd roaring denunciations at her, Jesus stooped down and began to doodle on the ground to show His indifference. Gently He cut her accusers down to her own level by telling them, "Let him who is without sin among you be the first to cast a stone at her." Then He doodled some more and they left, one by one, leaving Jesus and the woman alone together. And Jesus raising Himself said to her,

"Woman where are they? Has no one remained to condemn thee?" She said, "No one, Lord." Then Jesus said, "Neither will I condemn thee. Go thy way, and from now on sin no more."

Now the thing to be noted about these two cases is not just that Jesus forgave sin, that He obliterated guilt, but the way in which He did it. In each case He was careful to allay fear, embarrassment. In each case the sinner involved was in rather an emotional and social predicament. In each case He gently extricated the poor woman and calmed her down and restored her composure.

Christ's understanding of the psychological requirements of guilt feelings are also evidenced in the parable He told of the prodigal son. There could hardly be a more penetrating analysis of what these needs are. "But when he [the prodigal son] came to himself he said, 'How many hired men in my father's house have bread in abundance, while I am perishing here with hunger! I will get up and go to my father and will say to Him, Father I have sinned against heaven and before thee, I am no longer worthy to be called thy son; make me as one of thy hired men.' " In other words, when the prodigal son became contrite he spontaneously wanted to confess his failure to his father, await his father's decision, and suffer for his faithlessness.

The prodigal son was the perfect exemplification of every sinner. All sin is the seeking of our own will contrary to our Father's will, a search for false independence that leads us from our Father's house. But sin is not just a passing act like writing on the water. It is an act which changes our conscious selves; it is like jumping down a well—a simple action that has abiding results. It changes a man. He no longer lives at peace with God; he no longer lives at peace with self.

The first thing the sinner feels is a disparity between what he knows he really is and the self he knows he ought to be. He ceases to be one with self. His mind is filled with confusion for he has lost that sense of direction in life, that sense of knowing where he is going. The standards of right and wrong which he has lived by now rise up to accuse him. And that sense of security and confidence in controlling his feelings and his emotions disappears and he begins to feel helpless, like a leaf tossed around by the breeze. And all that he has said was evil and wicked and to be shunned, now, to his surprise, has a strange fascination for him. With dread he realizes that he also loves what he hates, enjoys the evil which he detests.

The sinner begins to feel no good, to feel unclean. The joy and cleanness he has known in following his conscience tells him, "I did it." Sadness at his state gives way to anger with himself. "What a fool I was!" "How many hired men in my father's house have bread in abundance, while I am perishing here with hunger!"

The sinner no longer lives at peace with God.

sinners delight **81**

Grace is gone. He no longer has the feeling of being accepted by God, of being in God's good graces. He no longer has the feeling of divine power within him which grace gives. In its stead he feels only the weight of a tremendous debt upon his shoulders and the disapproval of God. The omnipotent power which created him and saved him is now turned in wrath upon him. Insufferable loneliness and emptiness fill the heart. The prodigal son "went and joined one of the citizens of that country, who sent him to his farm to feed swine. And he longed to fill his belly with the pods the swine were eating, but no one offered to give them to him." The sinner is rejected.

The only thing that can relieve the sinner is confession, acceptance of penance and suffering. Until he can actually confess out loud, not only when alone, but especially before the one whom he has offended, the thing remains repressed. And being repressed it does not go away; it just gnaws away. There has to be a movement the opposite from repression and that is confession. As a matter of fact, every time there is a murder written up in the papers the police are pestered with people who come in confessing that they committed it. There is nothing particularly wrong with these people except that they cannot bring themselves to confess the right offenses. The feeling that they have to confess is highly normal. Suppose a person is visiting a friend who cherishes antique ash trays. He kicks one over while the host is upstairs. If he surreptitiously brushes the pieces under the rug, he is going to be ashamed to look his friend in the eye as long as he lives. He slinks out of the house and kicks himself as he goes down the street. He cannot really face his antique-loving friend until he gets up the courage to look him in the eye and tell him what happened to that old, out-of-date excuse for an ashtray.

But confession is just the start. The rejection that has occurred by sinning must be eliminated by the restoration of acceptance. If a fellow gets the icy stare from his fellow-sufferers at a tea party when he commits the social sin of dunking his cookies, he really does not restore his composure until he can win back their charmed smiles. When a boy becomes the subject of paternal wrath by using his father's straight-edge for whittling, he walks around with the "blues" until the father smiles and tells him it is all right again. The prodigal son wanted to be welcomed back by his father, maybe as a hired servant, but he just wanted to be welcomed back.

Finally, the pain that is sensed as a result of knowing that the real self does not match up to the ideal self, the sorrow that blurts out, "I'm no good," leads one to punish self, to desire to suffer to balance things up again. If a fellow has accidentally stabbed a brother with a knife or bashed him with some blunt instrument the resultant kick in the pants can be positively a relief. "Make me as one of thy hired men."

All of the gentle kindness that Jesus exercised in reassuring and restoring the bruised and guilty spirit of the woman who was a sinner in the city and the woman taken in adultery, Jesus exercises in the sacrament of Penance. All the understanding of the psychology of guilt that Jesus manifested in the parable of the prodigal son He utilized in the invention of the sacrament of Penance. It is a masterpiece in the art of healing the soul, because the medicine so beautifully suits the disease, the sacrament so perfectly fulfills the needs of the contrite sinner. If the parable of the prodigal son is the most beautiful short story ever told, then the sacrament of Penance is by equal right a masterpiece, a thing of beauty.

In the sacrament of Penance all the needs of the contrite sinner are satisfied. First, the need for honest admission, for getting it all off one's chest is satisfied in the act of confession. The faults and the failures that gnaw away in secret are brought to the surface where they can be dealt with rationally. These faults and failures are described in an honest and adequate manner, i.e., in terms of morality.

As for the need for a renewed sense of worthiness and acceptance, this is provided by absolution. The words of the priest not only restore grace to the soul, but the sinner can actually hear the words. After all, grace cannot be sensed. We can only be sure of its presence by faith and faith comes by hearing. The sinner is not just telling himself that everything is all right. A voice comes from outside himself. Absolution can never be as flimsy a thing as self-deception. Just as the ear that listened was an agent of the heavenly Father, so too the voice that absolves is armed with the power of God. The sinner can be sure that his wickedness is taken away by the passion and death of Jesus, and not by his own efforts or by the priest's kindliness. Hence the abolition of his wickedness is complete and total. It is not a matter of a psychiatrist listening in objective silence to a tale of woe and then rationalizing the whole affair to the point where a man with an inferiority complex is convinced that his complex is just as good as the next man's. It is a matter of a spiritual change taking place, a change that comes from God Himself, but certified by a voice that can actually be heard. The faithful sinner can be just as certain of his forgiveness as the woman who was a sinner in the city or the woman taken in adultery. The voice falls from different lips but the meaning and the power are the same.

Finally, there is provided for the sinner an opportunity to prove his willingness to suffer and to satisfy. A token penance is prescribed which enables him to relieve himself of the need for penalization. In ancient times it might have involved sitting at the church door dressed in sack-cloth and with ashes sprinkled on the head. But now-a-days it is more likely to be ten Our Fathers and ten Hail Marys. And these are not just a token that

God needs, but a token that the sinner needs. Ten Our Fathers and ten Hail Marys is less impressive than forty days at the church door in scratchy clothes and carbon, but the psychological point is identical.

Life without sin would be great. But granted that a man is a sinner, there is nothing greater than a good confession.

chapter nine

court of appeal

Many people, including Fathers of the Church, eminent theologians, and the Council of Trent, have noticed that confession has about it a certain resemblance to a courtroom. It is not very likely that many of these priests and bishops and cardinals had unpleasant skirmishes with the law; so it is not very likely that they found this resemblance unpleasant. But in our times even the most law-abiding motorist can fall quite unwittingly into the clutches of the gendarmes. The thought of a court appearance is not calculated to cheer the soul.

Now, if the Council of Trent says there is a resemblance between confession and a courtroom, the resemblance is there for sure. But it is unfair to Christ to think about confession as having the unpleasant aspects of a court. Confession is a sort of courtroom appearance but totally different in detail and over-all effect from the courts of justice with which we are more or less remotely familiar. And it is unfair to feel about confession the way we feel about the traffic court.

Police courts are usually drab and dingy. The Supreme Court is stately and dignified. But all courts are a little on the chill side. The judges look stern and impassive. The prosecuting attorneys look righteous and unpleasantly efficient. One after another witnesses point accusing fingers. Bit by bit the evidence piles up. The verdict comes and the sentence is passed and the culprit is turned over to the sheriff. He leaves the courtroom an outcast from society and exchanges his freedom for walls and bars. Newspapers plaster his picture and his guilt on the front page and load their copy with uncomplimentary adjectives. There is nothing very appealing about a court of justice, especially if you are guilty.

The circumstances of confession are much different. First of all there is nothing very public about it. A confessional is just a little booth in a church. Most confessionals are only a stone's throw from the Blessed Sacrament. The whole thing is very private. Nobody listens but the priest, and he never tells what he hears. The priest has the powers of the heavenly Father and usually a bit of His patience too. There are no prosecuting attorneys and no accusing witnesses. Every man accuses himself. As a matter of fact, nobody passes a verdict on his guilt except the guilty man himself. The sentences are light, ranging from three Hail Marys to a whole rosary. Only the most experienced sinners get more than a rosary. The penitent leaves the confessional an innocent man, restored to the society of the saints and reinstated as a child of God. He exchanges the slavery of sin for the freedom of the spirit, the prospect of maybe eternal punishment for the prospect of eternal beatitude. Confession is a court, but a court of mercy, not of justice. It is a court with lots of appeal.

Another feature of confession that many people find disquieting is uneasiness about what the priest thinks of us and our sins. Confidence comes hard when sympathy cannot be anticipated. Only a world-wide poll of hundreds of thousands of confessors could provide statistics on this subject. But that would hardly be possible because priests are notoriously difficult to pry information out of. And even if a worried penitent did have the statistics in his pocket there would always be the chance of running across the liverish one per cent.

Now there is going to be a certain amount of shame involved, regardless of what the priest thinks. Shame is never fun but it is unavoidable, a sort of minimum fee exacted of a contrite sinner. It is impossible to say what each and every priest thinks each and every time a person goes to confession. But some generalities about attitudes and thoughts are quite applicable. In the first place, the priest has been exposed to at least four years

court of appeal **89**

of moral theology during which time all of the logical possibilities of sinning were explored exhaustively. It is not likely that a penitent is going to take him by surprise. On top of this academic exposure to sin, the priest has listened to endless tales of woe which have been for the most part monotonously alike, since there are very few original sinners. In other words, experience leads him to take it for granted that human nature has a well-developed tendency toward sinning. Being acquainted with human nature as it really is, the chances are he will be quite objective in his thinking on the subject and not given to swooning. Our own inflamed tonsils can be tremendously important to us, but the doctor looks at them with at most an uninspired grunt. Doctors see too many tonsils to be expected to stand up and shout at the sight of ours. This attitude might be a little unflattering to one's own personal germ cultures as far as doctors are concerned, but in the case of confession it is quite comforting in a priest.

Remember, too, that the priest is a priest and for the most part thinks as a priest. Endless recitals of little venial sins and imperfections might dull his attention, especially if the day is warm and it is mid-afternoon. But the more serious the sin, the more thankful the priest is for his vocation. It is in those moments when he is absolving a really first-rate sinner that his life seems most worthwhile to him. And the bigger the sinner, the deeper is the priest's sense of the miraculous. For he knows that at the words of absolution a human heart is raised to life again just as truly as at the command of Christ, Lazarus came to life again. The same sense of awe that a priest has when, at the words of consecration which fall from his lips, ordinary bread and wine are changed into the Body and Blood of Christ, comes when, at the words of absolution, ordinary human sinners are changed into the Mystical Body of Christ. The miracle is much alike, and so is the sense of awe. And the frankness and courage and honesty that penitent sinners show in confessing their sins surprises him much more than their weakness in committing those sins.

This brings up another point. The priest does not make the moral law; he is bound to it just like everyone else. And when someone comes along groaning because the Lord does not make exceptions, the priest is going to groan, too, but for a different reason. The worst thing that could be done to a whiner is to pat him on the back. It just would not be charitable. And what holds for the groaner holds for the white-washer too. Sinning is bad enough but to whitewash and rationalize one's peccadilloes can be fatal. The worst thing that can be done with such a penitent is to sympathize with his lies. He will begin to believe them himself and wake up in hell wondering how on earth he ever got there. The priest does not want that to happen.

Another difficulty that people have with confession is the monotony of it all. Week after week, month after month, year after year the same old story and the same three Our Fathers and three Hail Marys. Really this is not a difficulty with confession but with the one confessing. On the one hand it is unfair to expect that each and every confession is going to be a tremendous spiritual experience. But on the other hand this monotony is an unhealthy symptom, a symptom usually found in people who do not do anything very bad, perhaps just gossip and give way to impatience and have distractions in their prayers. Normally a person should become holier as he grows older, and as he becomes holier his conscience should bother him more and more. In the normal picture, a beginner starts out worrying about mortal sins; his chief interest in the spiritual life is to keep out of that unhappy state. But as life goes on one's interests should broaden to the development of virtue and character. And as charity comes to full flower, interest should center more and more on just loving God and being united to Him. This means that there should be a corresponding delicacy of conscience about smaller things, a progress from worrying about mortal sins to worrying about venial sins, from worrying about not being humble enough to not trusting in God enough. After all, the deeper love develops between two people, the more out of place selfishness and lack of trust become. It is the same between the person and God. The man who keeps buying size three shoes from the time he is four till the time he is forty ought not to complain about the monotony of it all to the shoe company. Remember that we move toward God on the feet of desire. It is not the monotony of the same old impatience or the same old penance that gets so boring; rather it is the monotony of the same old smallness of desire.

This business of monotony brings up the question of how often a person should go to confession. The Jansenists used to think that infrequency made for peppier confessions. But the Jansenists were heretics. As a matter of fact, a Catholic does not have to go to confession each time he wishes to receive Holy Communion. The trick to it is avoiding all sin, which indeed is quite a trick. Mortal sinners naturally are obliged to go to confession before receiving the other sacraments. Hence, if Eastertime comes along and a Catholic is in the state of mortal sin, he is obliged to go to confession so that he can receive Holy Communion and fulfill his Easter duty. The same would be true if he were a candidate for Confirmation, Holy Orders, Matrimony, or Extreme Unction. This is a matter of legal obligation. Actually, a mortal sinner ought to flee to the confessional at the earliest possible moment and he ought to be careful to look both ways before crossing the street on the way to the church. Delay is a bad gamble. Then, too, once a person has fallen into mortal sin it is so easy to work on the idea of "might as well be hanged for a sheep as a lamb." Getting to confession promptly is the best protection from falling again, even if it means every day.

Most people lie in between these two extremes. They are not so holy as the Blessed Virgin nor so heinous as the daily wife-beater. When it comes to going to confession with only venial sins, one should go frequently enough to keep alive a habitual willingness to submit one's life to God's judgment. God is going to judge us anyway. The idea is to submit to it willingly while this judgment is still in terms of mercy; when death and justice come it will be too late. The church has made no legislation on how often it takes to keep alive this spirit as far as lay people are concerned. But the code of canon law says that monks and nuns should go once a week. Lay people do not have much better memories than monks and nuns. Once or twice a month certainly would not be overdoing this business of confession.

All the complaints about confession, all the problems about understanding confession, all the difficulties about what to say and how often to go can all be taken care of very simply. It all hinges around a sense of sinfulness. After all, a drowning man has no complaints about a life-preserver, no problems about its shape and construction, no difficulties about what to do with it.

A sense of sinfulness involves, first of all, an examination of conscience, which presupposes that there is more to conscience than the part that bothers us. That part does not need any examination. The part that needs to be examined obviously must be shrouded in a bit of obscurity, which is not surprising for nature has a tendency to shrink from the unpleasant.

To be really useful, this probing of conscience has to be realistic. It is not enough to take a big breath, furrow the brow, close the eyes, and repeat over and over again, "what a worm I am." An examination of conscience should deal with facts and put them in proper focus. There are some books on the market which are designed to assist in this matter. They are for the most part like shopping lists. Before confession the busy penitent can pick half a dozen of these and a peck of those, and, without half trying, dig up plenty of matter for the priest. But an examination of conscience that is going to promote a sense of sinfulness has to go deeper. Actually the process is a matter of comparison, and if you are going to compare two things you have to know both of them; otherwise it is like buying shoes from a grab-bag when you do not even know the size of your feet. The things to be compared are self and the standards to which we are supposed to conform. Where can one find these standards described? Well, the commandments more or less rough out the picture for us. But the commandments pick on very obvious types of hideousness and it takes a moral theologian to figure out how the fine points fit in. For example, "Thou shalt not steal" also includes "Thou shalt not peek into other people's mail," but one is not likely to know this without a semi-nary training. Then, too, one can get a list of the virtues; they also describe the standards. Faith, hope and charity cover a broad field in three words. Eutrapalia, gnome, and synderesis do not make much sense to the ordinary garden variety of sinner. Lists of virtues have the disadvantage of being too abstract for the purposes of comparison. Even a moral theologian is not too likely to ask himself before confession how he is doing with eutrapalia.

Perhaps the best way to make the comparison is to use the life of Christ and the preachings of Christ. After all, Christ is our model and example. We have a rather complete description of His personality in the Gospels wherein we find that He lived up to the letter of the beatitudes. God Himself in looking at us is always making comparisons; He compares us to Christ. If we are going to know ourselves from God's point of view, we had better make the same comparisons. "I am not like the rest of men" was the Pharisee's examination of conscience, and he did not return to his home justified. Perhaps the Gospels are obscure on some points, especially on dogmatic points. But when it comes to an example of how we should live, every-thing is abundantly clear. A familiarity with the Gospels is indispensable to the development of a sense of our own failure. This familiarity cannot be acquired three minutes before confession. It must be a lifetime occupation.

Self is the other half of the comparison. Really it is self that presents the problem. For some strange reason, our real self is the last thing in the world we know. Self-knowledge requires, first of all, daily attention. A few minutes before we go to sleep spent in reviewing the events of the day is a prime requisite. A recollection of the whole of one's life is the second requisite. After all, life is like a snow ball rolling down a hill; it is an accumulative process. What we are today is the result of what we have been doing since the ripe old age of three or four. Temper tantrums at thirty-eight are a hold-over from the same defense mechanism that was popular at eight.

Once self-knowledge is acquired and one becomes rather familiar with the personality of Christ, a sense of sinfulness comes naturally and spontaneously. The only other factor that has to be added is the passion and death of Jesus. Subtle and abstract as the human intelligence might be, only the passion and death of Jesus can reveal how serious sin is in God's sight. And unless we see ourselves from God's point of view we never see ourselves as we really are. For that matter we are not too likely to see God, either.

Some people claim that confession makes sinning easy. How wrong they are! Sinning has never been hard. The only thing that confession makes easy is forgiveness.

really dramatic

Perhaps the best place to begin talking about the Eucharist is the Mass. After all, that is where the Eucharist begins. As far as religious ceremonies in the Catholic Church are concerned, the Mass is long and complicated. As far as books and explanations of the Mass are concerned, they are also usually long and complicated. In a way this is only right and proper, for the Mass celebrates a tremendous mystery and the processes of appreciating a mystery are long and complicated. None the less, the following explanation of the Mass is going to be short and simple. Maybe it will fall short of the mark. On second thought *maybe* is the wrong word; *certainly* would perhaps be better.

The Mass is a drama so its explanation necessarily involves drama. Suppose you were attending one of those skits or plays that schools quite frequently stage about the time of George Washington's birthday. They are an opportunity for the dramatic class to show off and at the same time they do help to promote patriotism and an appreciation of history. The stage is set for Valley Forge: snow, trees, and a little fire. The cast is equipped with bedraggled blue uniforms, three-cornered hats, and muskets. Now suppose that a south-sea islander fresh off a trans-Pacific airplane came into the auditorium and you were appointed to explain the whole thing to him so he could appreciate what was going on. Of course he would be puzzled about the strange language, the peculiar clothes, and the meaningless movements of the actors. What is the absolute minimum of information he would have to have before he could appreciate what was going on and feel some of the patriotic spirit the play is supposed to stimulate? He would not have to know English. He would not have to read reams of American colonial history. He would not have to listen to endless lectures and make extensive research in museums about early American costumes. All that you would have to tell him is that this was a play, a representation of something that happened in history, and what went on in the mind and heart of the main character—that George Washington was a man fighting for the freedom and independence of a new nation. That would be sufficient.

Suppose the same sun-tanned character walked into Mass one fine Sunday morning. He would see a man standing in front of a table flanked by two small boys who rangs bells with industry and did no small amount of fidgeting. The man at the table would be dressed in strange clothes, speak an unknown language, and would bob up and down and walk back and forth in an apparently pointless fashion. Suppose, further, that you were appointed to explain the whole thing to this man so that he could appreciate what was going on and begin to feel something of what the Mass is supposed to stir up in the heart of man. Of course, it would be in church and you would have to economize on your words. What is the basic minimum that you would have to tell him? Well, he would not have to know anything about the history of the liturgy, the Gregorian sacramentary, the gradual Psalms, and the Mozarabic Rite. He would not even have to know Latin with its conjugations and its declensions. You would not even have to tell him the names of all the vestments and the sequence of all of the parts of the Mass. It would be enough if he knew that it was a drama, a representation of the greatest moment in history, and what went on in the mind and heart of the leading character—that He was the Son of God laying down His life for the salvation of sinners. That is all you would have to explain, and the visitor could begin to feel something of the spirit of sacrifice that the Mass is supposed to evoke.

This example gives a general sketch of what the

Mass is. As a matter of fact, the example is nothing but window-dressing put on the catechism definition which says that the Mass is the re-enactment of the sacrifice of Calvary in an unbloody manner. But there are highlights that make this drama especially interesting.

In the first place, no play about George Washington can bill George as playing himself in the leading role. In the Mass Christ does just that. He is really present in the two leading roles—victim and priest. He is really present as the victim because He is really present under the physical appearances of the consecrated bread and wine offered in sacrifice. This presence is just as real as His presence upon the cross of Calvary. True, the suffering has stopped, but the sufferer is present none the less. Christ having died once, can die no more; but once a savior always a savior. Furthermore, Christ is really present in the priest, though the priest himself is just His instrument. The priest has the power to change bread and wine into the Body and Blood of Christ. This is a very real power. Yet it is a power that the priest does not exercise independently and in his own right, the way he might digest his dinner. It is Christ working in and through the priest. Really, there is only one priest and one priesthood. The reverend fathers are merely sharers in the priesthood of Christ. Thus Christ is really present in both the leading roles.

Christ the victim is both signified and present

under the physical appearances of bread and wine. Christ the priest is both signified and present in the priest who pronounces the words of consecration. The separate consecration of the bread and wine signifies the death of Christ on the cross when His body and blood were separated. This is the very heart of the Mass, the very instant of sacrifice. After all, if the death of Jesus was a sacrifice, then the representation of that death is also a sacrifice. If my mother came from Ireland, I can say she is Irish. I can say the same about her picture. But there is one thing to note about this death of Christ: the death is only signified in the separate consecration; it is not really happening. Christ having died once, can die no more. Still, there is something about this representation that should not be glossed over. Though the death is not actually re-occurring, the effects actually brought about by this death are. Christ still lives to make intercession for us. And while Mass is celebrated the reparation, the propitiation, the salvation wrought on Calvary are actually happening.

When Deems Taylor goes about explaining a musical masterpiece he usually mentions what toil and sacrifice the composer suffered in turning it out. For example, the fact that the composer had fifteen children and had to work as a plumber's helper during the day and had to do his composing after his family went to bed, gives us a better appreciation of his music. We appreciate it more knowing the suffering that was involved in its production. We appreciate it more knowing something of the motivation which moved the artist, his passionate desire to create something beautiful to charm future generations. Now, the drama of the Mass was written by Christ and it was written with His blood. No other artist has ever put his very life into his work. Other artists toil and sacrifice because they feel the urge to create, or to leave behind them things of beauty for all posterity. But no artist has ever so loved posterity that he would lay down his life to save it. And no artist's love for mankind has been so fruitful as Christ's. His sacrifice not only brings into being a thing of beauty to rejoice the heart of man; His sacrifice brings into being the Eucharist to sanctify the heart of man.

Quite a few people wake up on Sunday morning either out of habit, or because the offspring have sprung and are making noise with the funnies, or because the alarm rings about eleven-thirty and the groan is heard, "Sunday again, and I have to go to Mass." In other words, sometimes the chief motivation for attendance is a sense of obligation, of more or less unpleasant obligation. In church itself the looks on many people's faces are very inspiring. They look almost as if they were in heaven. But they are only some of the people. In any church during Sunday Mass you can find quite a few who are bored to tears, who spend their time inspecting millinery or twirling

really dramatic **103**

rosaries. Now these things are not just impolite, like blowing bubble gum at the opera; they are a pity. They indicate an inability to appreciate what is going on up front.

Multitudinous efforts are made to give these drab souls some appreciation of the Mass, but the efforts are not notoriously successful. Some people seem to think that what would do the trick is a knowledge of Latin, as if the Latin language had some sacramental value. The priest knows differently. He has most of his distractions in Latin. Old Cicero himself would tell you that Latin is not enough. Others think that the best way to attend Mass is to say the rosary, which is the poor man's breviary. That may well be, but the constitutions for most religious orders say that the Office is not to be chanted during Mass. Granted that the rosary is a good thing, a very good thing, but it is not as good as the Mass. Just because you are saying the rosary well it does not follow that you are attending Mass well, though of course it certainly is better than rubber-necking. Still other physicians of liturgical lethargy suggest that all would be well if the congregation would answer the responses at Mass or sing at least the every-day parts or as a basic minimum read the English missal. These suggestions do have a lot of value. The text of the Mass and the music of the Mass were never meant to be a personal devotion of the priest or the private prerogative of a few devout but vocally underprivileged females. The words and the music of the Mass were invented for the masses just like the Mass itself. Missals and music help a lot but they do not come to the heart of the matter directly. Or perhaps it would be better to say they presuppose that appreciation has already begun and merely promote it.

Basic appreciation of the Mass is very simple. It involves faith and understanding of the fact that the Mass is a drama, a re-enactment; it is also a representation of what went on in the mind and heart of Jesus at that moment. The drama part is fairly easy to think through. The mind and heart of the Savior are fathomless. But to the degree that one can see with what spirit of worship Jesus offered Himself up to the Father, so much the more spontaneous and vehement will be the movement of one's own heart in the same spirit. After all, this is not a peculiar sort of thing. We do it every time we go to the movies. The fears, the joys, the anxieties of the hero are ours. We live through the drama with him. Basically that is all one is supposed to be doing at Mass.

Appreciating the Mass involves more than leather-bound missals, but costs less. It involves more than singing Gregorian chant, but is not restricted to the musically gifted. Appreciation of the Mass presupposes meditation, discovery, personally thinking things through. Meditation is different from reading; discovery is different from listening. At best, reading and listening are preliminary to meditating. Meditating is like digesting; it makes something part of us. Reading and listening are more like eating. Feeding is a thing that can be done by bottle, spoon or hypo. Digesting is a thing we have to do for ourselves. The essentials of the Mass have to be meditated on before the Mass becomes a part of us, or to phrase it more accurately, we become a part of the Mass.

Quite likely just about everyone is going to day-dream and twirl a rosary once in a while during Mass. But the man who comes to Mass his whole life through only out of a sense of obligation, who has never thrilled at the words of consecration, wept at the thought of how much Christ loves us, nor lost himself in this surge of worship to the Father—that man is dead but not buried. He is dead to the fact that he is a sinner and a member of a sinful race in need of redemption, and so is not impressed by a Redeemer. He is dead to the truth that he is a creature in need of everything as he stands before his Creator, a creature who has received all he has from his Creator. Such a man is dead in the heart and dead in the head, just as dead as the day the clods echo on his coffin.

The Mass is the re-enactment of the sacrifice of Christ on Calvary. And we can be reasonably sure that if we are bored to tears at Mass, our tears on Calvary would have been from boredom too.

real presents

The key to an appreciation of the sacraments is to consider them as Christ's artistic masterpieces. The key to an appreciation of the Eucharist is to view it as a masterpiece in the art of love. The Eucharist comes into being as an effect of Christ's love for men, love even unto death. The Eucharist, as it exists among us on the altar, is a gesture of love—a gift from lover to beloved. The Eucharist as it affects our lives leads us to love Christ more vehemently.

Gestures of love and gifts have to serve two purposes if they are going to amount to anything. After all, love involves at least two people. In the first place the gesture and the gift are going to have to be expressive of the love of the lover. It is for this reason that young men in love wrack their brains in writing their letters and consult various dictionaries, books of synonyms, and poets.

It is for this reason that their birthday and Christmas shopping takes such a long time. The perfect gesture of love, the perfect gift not only expresses perfectly the feelings of the lover and the giver but in some way fills a need in the beloved. In selecting a gift, a lover tries to find something that is desired so that when the box is opened she will exclaim, "Oh, it is just the thing I wanted!" Hence, a man does not give his mother a box of cigars for Mother's Day, nor does a priest's mother give him a neck-tie for Christmas. In the Eucharist there are two sets of properties or characteristics: some of them are very wonderful and some of them are very humble. All that is wonderful and mysterious and filled with majesty in the Eucharist belongs to the sacrament, as it is the perfect expression of the love of Jesus. All that is humble and simple and ordinary, like daily bread, belongs to the sacrament, as it is tailored to fulfill our needs and requirements.

First consider the Eucharist as an expression of Christ's love for us, as His gift to us. Now there is nothing more obvious about lovers than the fact that they like to be in each other's presence. When a boy begins to find himself attracted to some young lady, he offers to carry her school books for her. It is not a question of his thinking that she is physically handicapped, but just an excuse to be with her. A man really in love with his wife and family just cannot wait to get home from work. And if a husband is gone seven nights a week, the first complaint the wife makes is "he doesn't love me any more." If it is necessary that lovers be separated, they try to bridge the gap with photographs, letters, and telephone calls. Love tends toward presence, and the more real the presence the better. A telephone call is better than a letter, and a visit in person is better than a picture.

Christ in His love for us wanted to be present to us. Hence, in the Eucharist He has contrived a way to burst asunder the bonds of time and place and be really and physically present to each and every one of us all through the ages and all through the world. Thus it is that we speak of the Eucharist as the Real Presence. Without this miracle He would have been restricted to walking and talking to a relatively small group of people for just a few years. The Scripture commentators make note of this when they come to explain that phrase of Saint John the Evangelist, "and dwelt amongst us." The Greek word that John used meant "pitched his tent amongst us." Obviously John had in mind a nomadic sort of existence where people lived in tents. After all, the Jews had been a nomadic people for many centuries. In the Eucharist Christ dwells in what we call a tabernacle. Now the word tabernacle means tent. In other words, He has pitched His tent amongst us. He is still as really present among us as He was in the family home in Nazareth or in the upper room with the Apostles during the Last Supper. He lives in a house just down the street from each and every one of us. He has an address in the phonebook in every village and town.

There is another interesting thing about this Real Presence. All the other sacraments are passing things like a smile. The sacred reality of the sacrament of Baptism exists only while the water is being poured and the words are being pronounced. The sacrament of Penance exists only while the words of absolution are whispered over a penitent sinner. But because of Christ's desire to be present to us in the sacred reality of the Eucharist, it is a sacrament we can keep in our churches day and night. His presence is permanent. The Eucharist is the only sacrament in which the sacred reality is an enduring thing.

But love tends not only to presence, it tends also to union. A young mother gravitates toward the cradle where her infant lies. She tends toward presence. But despite the doctor's advice she soon picks the baby up and holds the child to her bosom. Lovers are not content to sit at opposite ends of the sofa. So, too, Christ's love for us tends not only to presence and Real Presence but also to union. He is not content to be looked at across the communion rail. He is not content to be at opposite ends of the same room. Hence, this sacrament is a thing which becomes united to us. It is the one sacrament, as a matter of fact, that we even receive inside ourselves. It is not just a question of union in the sense of a handshake, but of something much more intimate. We receive Christ physically within ourselves as spiritual food. He becomes immediately united to our wills. And of this presence or union, St. Augustine said, "He is closer to us than we are to ourselves."

There is another point about gifts that make them expressive of love. You must have noticed that when a girl gives her boy friend a pair of argyle socks for Christmas, she often does not go to the store to buy a pair, she knits them herself. Of course, they do not turn out the same size, and maybe she drops a few stitches here and there and gets the pattern mixed up. They are definitely different from store-bought argyles. But this is just what makes them an appropriate gift. She has managed to impress her personality on her gift. The really personal gifts are things we make ourselves, and they are more appropriate if we impress our personalities upon them. Christ has managed to impress His personality on His gift. At the beginning it is just bread and wine. But in the process of preparing it for us He enters so thoroughly into His gift, He impresses Himself so completely upon His gift, that there is no substance of bread and wine left but only their appearances. He completely transforms the bread and wine into Himself by that tremendous miracle which we know as transubstantiation.

In the foregoing examples we have seen how Christ has imitated the processes of human love in preparing the gift which expresses His love for us. There comes a point, however, when we have to leave aside the analogies drawn from human love and use divine love as our example. Remember that God's love works just the opposite from human love. Human love is always a response to goodness, real or imagined. We love a person because he or she is lovable, because he or she either is or appears to us to be the most beautiful, the most handsome, and the most charming person in the world. On the other hand, God's love is not responsive but creative. He does not love things because they are good. Things are good because He loves them. When God's love comes into play creation happens. His will unleashes His omnipotence. There is an aspect of the Eucharist in which this creative characteristic of divine love is found. Theologians have a fancy Latin term to express it: *ex opere operato*. Frequently this point comes up when they have to explain the difference between sacraments and sacramentals. Sacramentals, like holy water and blessed ashes, persuade us to be holy. Holy water works only according to the feelings of devotion one has in using holy water. The Eucharist does not just persuade us to be holy, it makes us holy. The Eucharist does not work depending upon our feelings as we use the sacrament. It works like food. It is not that a man smacks his lips, or that his eyes light up and his mouth waters which makes his meal effective. Nourishment and added pounds result, not from his feelings or devotion to food, but from the nourishing power in the food itself.

The sacrament of the Eucharist works like food; it is effective and not just persuasive. It is effective because God's love and Christ's love are not just persuasive and responsive, but creative and effective.

Remember, we noted that the perfect gift is not only expressive of the lovers' feelings, it also has to be useful. In selecting a gift a lover tries to find something that is needed, so that when the box is opened the one loved will exclaim, "Oh it's just the thing I wanted." Hence I don't give my mother cigars and she does not give me neck-ties for Christmas. All the tremendous reality of the Eucharist is visible only to the eyes of faith, for it is an expression of Christ's love, of His feelings for us. The humble side of the Eucharist, the simple appearances that meet the eye, are designed to meet our needs.

What is it that we need most in this life? Remember that we are wayfarers, that this life is a trial where we learn to know and love God at a distance so that vision will be a thing we have merited. The most fundamental thing we need in this time of trial, then, is the merit of faith. Faith is the opposite of vision; it is assent to the unseen, and hence it takes a push from the will. This element of a voluntary push because there is no evidence to meet the eye is what makes faith meritorious. Remember that faith is the most fundamental act, the process of moving toward God. Remember, too, that it was not because the doubting Thomas saw the risen Christ that he was blessed. Christ said, "Blessed are those who have not seen and have believed." The Apostles and contemporaries of Christ could see and touch the humanity of Christ. It was obvious in the fact that He ate, He slept, He argued, and He wept. What they could not see and had to believe in was His divinity, the fact that He was also God. In Christ, the Son of God was hypostatically united to frail human nature, the God-head was present in the form of a man. In the Eucharist, not only the divinity but also the humanity of Christ is present under the humble appearances that meet the eye and the sense of touch. Hence, in this sacrament we have the merit of belief, not only in His divinity like the Apostles, but also in His humanity. In a way our faith is greater.

The second greatest need we have is that we be taught by God. And the most important truth that we need to be taught and constantly reminded of, is that in Adam all men have sinned and in Christ all men are saved. Hence, granted that Christ was going to present even His humanity in this sacrament but shrouded under appearances, it was appropriate that He choose appearances that should somehow remind us of the fall of Adam. Thus, the appearances of this sacrament are the appearances of food, that we might remember that it was by eating of the forbidden fruit of the tree of the knowledge of good and evil that mankind fell from God's pleasure, and that it is by eating of this bread of life that we become again close friends of God.

Of course, if this sacrament had the appearances of an apple, the allusion to the disaster in the garden of Eden might be more literal. But it would be less significant and more inconvenient. In the first place, apples are not found generally all over the world. They grow in some places and they do not grow in others. Bread and wine are much more common and easier to get. And although the apple would be a more literal reminder of the fall of Adam, the appearances of bread and wine are a much better reminder of the salvation which comes through Christ. They signify, in a way that an apple never could, the separation of Christ's body and blood on Calvary, that this sacrament is the fruit of His loving Sacrifice.

Christ put unfathomable wisdom and ingenuity into this gesture of His love for each and every one of us. It is a masterpiece. The physical laws of nature He just brushed aside as interfering with His work of love. It is only as a gesture of Christ's love for us that we can really understand the Eucharist.

In this business of love, understanding is important. Without it, the Hottentot misunderstands the kiss. Without the ability to see that the argyle socks are obviously a work of love, one is likely to say the wrong thing and put an end to a budding romance. The art of love-making requires intelligence on both sides: on the side of inventing the gesture and on the side of receiving the gesture.

Yet there is more to the business of love than understanding. Understanding is not enough; it is only a small part of the process of appreciating a gift from a lover. No matter how well we understand, we really do not appreciate a gift unless we love the giver in the first place.

the big moment

In external occupations, like playing golf, there is a measurable external standard against which the player can gauge his score. If the golfer plays the course at par, he goes home happy. If he does better than par, he throws a party. If he does less than par, he either invents excuses or takes a few lessons. With psychological experiences, this is less common. There is no numerical standard by which we can gauge our appreciation of an opera, i.e., whether we got out of it what a man should get out of it. If everyone else raves about the performance and we have been bored to tears, we might shrug our shoulders in plebeian resignation, climb on the band wagon and do a little hypocritical raving of our own, or borrow a book on opera and try to discover what it is all about.

Going to Communion is not an external occupation like playing golf. There is no numerical par for measuring our response to the event. And generally people do not leave church after Communion raving about how it moved them. None the less, there are certain standards by which most people compare their experiences in receiving Communion. Quite a few feel hypocritical walking back from the rail with eyes modestly cast down and hands piously folded. Quite a few more feel under par reading a thanksgiving after Communion out of a prayer book. Unconsciously or half-consciously, most of us have some standard by which we measure our psychological experiences in going to Communion.

How, then, do we form these standards? Quite likely most people who go to Communion have in the back of their minds some ideas that go back to childhood when they were being prepared for their first Communion and the Sisters told them about Napoleon. The usual story is that Bonaparte was asked while in exile what was the biggest moment in his life. He answered, "My first Communion." The Sisters do a good thing in telling seven-year-olds that their first Communion is the biggest thing in life. But children are very impressionable and imaginative. They build up things out of proportion in their own minds. Adult Christmases are never like childhood Christmases. And so it is with Communion. Many people try to recapture the joy of their first Communion and imitate that childhood experience. But there usually lurks in the back of the mind a sense of failure. The trouble is that they have quite likely been measuring their present experiences against an un-real standard. It is not too likely that seven-year-olds will set the pace for the course. They are too impressionable, too easily stirred to deep enthusiasms. Children are wonderful but they are not paragons of adult religious behavior.

Then, too, most prayer books have formulae which are alleged to be appropriate for use after Communion. These formulae are invariably on the fervent side. They generally have such phrases as: "Dear bleeding heart of Jesus, my heart bleeds for love of Thee." But it hardly seems appropriate to read out of a book at a time like that. After all, when a man embraces his wife he does not pull out a little book from his pocket and read to her. Then, too, there are no antecedent presumptions in favor of the authors of prayer books that would establish them as the criteria in a psychological inquiry.

Unquestionably there is a difficulty in establishing an objective norm as to what our experience in Communion should be like. In explaining the Mass and the Real Presence, analogies are possible. The only analogy that would be valid with respect to Holy Communion would be union with God in the beatific vision. In the Gospels we have only one phrase which is to the point: "He who eateth my body and drinketh my blood, abideth in me and I in him." The word "abide" is unquestionably pregnant with meaning. St. Thomas has written a prayer which also has significance in this matter: "O Sacred Banquet, in which Christ is received, the memory of His Passion is renewed, the mind is filled with grace, and a pledge of future glory is given to us." The word which is of interest is "pledge." The dictionary also has another word which translates the Latin of St. Thomas as "earnest"; the word is defined as: "a token or installment of what is to come." Unfortunately, a token or installment of what is to come is understandable only in terms of what is to come. In this present case the beatific vision is the less known factor. So, whereas it makes a magnificent foundation for an analogy, the analogy nevertheless teaches us very little at the present moment.

But generally in psychological matters we hold that the personal experience should in some way be proportionate to what objectively happens. What actually happens should condition what we feel. After all, if a man is telling you about a little girl who was run over by a truck and bursts out laughing in the middle of the story, you think he is peculiar and feel inclined toward the wisdom of commitment proceedings. Hence, a description of what actually, objectively happens in Holy Communion should provide a clue to what the appropriate experience should be.

Communion is a vital and conscious union between the soul and Christ. By the very nature of things, this sacrament cannot be received while the subject is asleep or unconscious. This consciousness of union is based upon faith rather than upon feeling. Friends consciously in contact are said to commune. The cake is united to the frosting but does not commune with it. Furthermore, this union is vital, not static; there is a passage of power in this union. Jesus always spoke of this sacrament as the Bread of Life.

As a matter of fact the term, "Bread of Life," is most appropriate for explaining the vital union of the soul and Christ. Food is united to us when we eat it, not only in terms of physical proximity, but in terms of vital reality. Food proves to be a source of energy and a source of satisfaction. In Holy Communion Jesus is united to the soul in two ways: as a source of grace and help, and as a source of joy and happiness, since it is a sample of heaven. Theologians have a neat, scientific way of expressing this truth. They say that Christ is united to us as an efficient and as a final cause. A thing that moves us to desire or provides happiness and satisfaction is a final cause.

The analogy of food is helpful in explaining the union of Christ and the Christian in Holy Communion, but like all analogies this one, too, has points where it does not fit. As Saint Augustine noted, we change food into ourselves when we eat. But in this eating, Christ, who is the food, changes us into Himself. Just as this sacrament comes into being by a complete change of the substance of bread and wine into the substance of Christ, so, too, in its reception it completely changes the human heart from loving self to loving God.

This analogy also limps on another point. The food we eat is united physically to us. As a matter of fact, it enters rather extensively into the body since it is carried by the blood stream to all the cells. Yet the food we eat only touches the body, it does not touch the soul. On the other hand the Bread of Life touches our will, our heart, and moves up to greater love. Only God and the Blessed Sacrament can move the will of man.

Finally, we do not love food the way we love a friend, and we do not delight in food the way we delight in a friend. We like food, we do not love food. In the sacrament of the Eucharist, Christ is the source of delight the way a friend is the source of happiness.

The effort at describing the appropriate psychological experience which corresponds to this reality involves an element of human conjecture. Yet this conjecture is well-founded. If you see a man drowning and throw him a life preserver, the element of conjecture that enters into your understanding of his feelings during the process is well-founded. It might be helpful to break our experience as regards the Holy Eucharist down into three moments: the state of the soul in the moment of approach to this union, the moment of union itself, and the aftermath of union.

Ideally, at the moment of approach to Holy Communion the soul should be filled with a desperate ache, an ache that comes from contradiction. It is not a contradiction in the sense that there is a desire to be united with Christ opposed by a desire to be separated from Him, as the man might suffer contradiction in his feelings as he stands at the edge of a swimming pool—liking the water but not the cold. It is more a contradiction in the sense that all one's efforts are frustrated and contradicted. For example, there is in the heart of man an emptiness, an abysmal loneliness which is in reality a desire for God. But it is the lot of most men that they try to fill the void with things other than God, with creature love, with creature comfort. Yet such efforts never fill the void nor comfort the loneliness; such efforts are contradicted and frustrated. Very few turn originally and consistently to God. For most men the pursuit of God follows upon the failure of other loves. Most men find out the hard way that they were made for God. For most men, as for St. Augustine, the cry, "My heart was made for thee, O Lord, and it is restless until it rests in Thee," is wrung from a heart painfully disillusioned. Somehow, unless this painful process has been experienced, most of us do not long desperately for Communion. Another example of how this sense of need for Communion is born of contradiction can be cited from the field of sin. There is consciousness of self-love, of self-centeredness in all one's thoughts, of self-seeking in all one's desires. Coupled to this insight is a consciousness of complete inadequacy to be otherwise, of an inability to get out of the quagmire of one's own ego. This awareness lives side by side with the realization that only God can fill the void in the human soul, that God is unspeakably more real and more lovable than our capacity for feeling and loving. This moment of approach might be characterized by St. Paul's cry, "Miserable man that I am, who shall deliver me from this body of contradiction. For the good that I would, I do not, and that which I would not, that I do."

In Christ's lifetime many people approached Him. The children ran spontaneously and without self-consciousness to Him. The Apostles harkened to an invitation; they welcomed the Messias of long expectation. Others sought Him out in desperation. The woman who was a sinner in the city, and whom we usually refer to as Mary Magdalene, sought Him out even in the house of a Pharisee, impelled by a need for true love, disillusioned by the emptiness of false love. The man who was covered with leprosy and fell at the feet of Jesus with the cry, "If thou wilt, thou can make me clean," was desperate or he would not have broken the law to approach so close to a non-leper. Perhaps some approach the Communion rail as spontaneously and innocently as the children in the Gospel. But it is the lot of most of us to approach with desperation as shown by Mary Magdalene and the leper.

In terms of this type of approach, the moment of union or of Communion should be filled with acceptance, appreciation, and exaltation. There should be a sense of acceptance or of receiving power from Christ, the power to get out of self and to give self to God. This sense of receiving should be a real experience—not like the sleeping beggar who accepts a dime in his cup, but like the drowning man who clutches at the lifeline. There should be a sense of appreciation, the sincere feeling that nothing else really matters, that no sacrifice is too big a price for this possession, that all else in this world is valueless without Christ. There should be a sense of admiration—not "how lucky I am," but "how wonderful God is"; a sense of belonging to Him, of being completely His. Finally, there should be exaltation, a feeling of power and permanence in His love, a feeling of "I am sure that neither death, nor life, nor angels, nor principalities, nor things present, nor things to come, nor powers, nor height, nor depth, nor any other creature will be able to separate us from the love of God which is in Christ, Jesus, Our Lord."

As for the aftermath of union, again the words of Saint Paul provide the clue. No one has described the influence of charity upon the human psyche more beautifully than St. Paul. "Charity is patient, is kind; charity does not envy, is not pretentious, is not puffed up, is not ambitious, is not selfseeking, is not provoked; thinks no evil, does not rejoice over wickedness but rejoices with the truth, bears with all things, believes all things, hopes all things, endures all things."

One might better have based the description of the psychology of Holy Communion on the experiences of the saints. Yet there is a tendency to think of the experiences of the saints as being a bit above us, something out of the reach of the common man. As a matter of fact, the description given above will in all probability be criticized as being out of reach. Most people will quite likely complain that such an experience does not come spontaneously to them. The thing to do is not to say that the experiences of the saints or the expectations of theologians are too high, but to inquire why our own lives are so low, and what can be done about it.

In the first place, the ability to receive Communion as it ought to be received is a gift. And like all gifts from God, it is ours for the asking. Unfortunately, however, this is one gift we seldom think of asking for.

In the second place, the best preparation for Communion is Communion. Other food takes away our appetite. This Food increases it. If a man says that he does not need to go to Communion, that he does not feel drawn to it, that he has no hunger for the Bread of Life, he is the man who needs it the most. He is the man who is on the brink of spiritual starvation. On the other hand, the reception of Holy Communion increases charity, and one of the most prominent functions of charity is to long for union with God. Hence, the more one receives of this sacrament the more one hungers for it.

Finally, preparation for Communion cannot be just ten minutes of reading beforehand. A few prayers and a few pages out of a book only put a thin veneer on our conscious selves. A few moments of reading a prayer book cannot lay aside deep-seated habits of thought, cannot provide certitude and conviction. The real preparation for Communion has to be the fruit of personal discovery, of a lifetime of pondering. It is not enough to read in a book that the human heart is an abyss of loneliness without God. One has to discover that truth personally by introspection and experience. It is not enough to read about the futility of all earthly joys to fill the void. One must have discovered by living that all created goods turn to ashes, that advertisements are false. It is not enough to read that we are helpless to break the chains of self-love and smallness. Only the man who has struggled in vain knows what it is to be helpless. It is not enough to read in a book that God is all-good. One must be haunted by the vision of His goodness which lies beyond the grasp of man in this life.

At the time of first Communion this awareness would be an anachronism. During life this awareness comes only to those who use their heads. But when the finger of death is upon us, this awareness will come easily. As the Irish poet wrote, "Please, God, do not let me die till Christ's Body in me lie."

chapter thirteen

God's name too

In the Western Church it is rare that a married man becomes a priest, for the law requires that the wife be buried either in a grave or in a cloister. It has been the experience of the Western Church that both Matrimony and the priesthood are full-time jobs which require a specialization of labor. We know St. Peter had a mother-in-law, but this is quite likely the exception which proved the rule.

There is one point, however, where parenthood and priesthood do come together. They both fit into God's plan in the same way. God invented both for the same reason. The arguments for their necessity are parallel. We can argue to the necessity of the other sacraments from the experiences of this life—our need to be born again, fed, nurtured, and repaired. But to arrive at the ultimate reason for the existence of Matrimony and Holy Orders, we have to turn our gaze from the experiences of this world to the nature of God in heaven. For God could well have made the whole human race Himself by the same action which brought Adam and Eve into existence, and He could well have saved the human race Himself without any human instrumentality. God can do without help. As a matter of fact, He dealt with the angels that way. They were all created in one instant. There are no boy and girl angels. And they all succeeded or failed in one instant; there were no sermons or confessions. God brought the angels into existence and into heaven without help. For God, all creation is superfluous, and that applies especially to parents and priests.

The catechism says that God made us to know Him and love Him and serve Him in this world and be happy with Him forever in heaven. That kind of an answer assigns the reason for which we exist. Men, on the one hand, are made to know and love God the way the eye was made to see and the cake was made to be eaten and chairs are made to be sat on. But why did the carpenter make the chair? Why did mother make the cake? And why did God make us? Our answer, on the other hand, can assign the motive which moved the carpenter and the cook. The carpenter made the chair to make money. Mother made the cake because she loves us. In other words, the questions are ambiguous. They can be answered either with the purpose of the product in mind or the motive of the producer. The first answer says what we are for after we are made; the second answer, why we were made at all.

God's purpose or motive in creating the world could not be gain. He did not suffer boredom and need the world as a plaything. It was not like the carpenter wanting to acquire money, or the mother wanting to acquire satisfaction. It was not a question of acquiring happiness; it was a question of God being abundantly happy in Himself and, because of this, pouring Himself out in the act of creation. Sometimes we speak of this as God manifesting His glory.

This pouring out of self whereby God creates has two meanings. It gives the motive for creation, and it gives the pattern for creation. God's glory is said to consist in manifesting Himself; *creation* reflects the beauty of the creator. The everlasting mountains proclaim His eternity. The sea, in its incessant pounding, proclaims His power. The eyes of little children proclaim His purity. God shared with creation all the facets of His beauty, all His characteristics and attributes to the extent that it is possible.

Among all the attributes of God, there is one which has specially endeared itself to mankind. Perhaps it is because this attribute involves us personally. Perhaps it is because its participation is so dear to us. This attribute is summarized in the one word, "Fatherhood." This attribute of Fatherhood adds to the idea of creation the idea of care and providence, of kindly governance. It is something like a king sharing with his son not only his good looks but also his kingship. Philosophers say this in the formula: God shared not only His nature but His causality.

This causality is shared by the plants which produce seeds, by the fish and the birds which generate offspring, by the fire which cooks eggs, by the carpenter, the painter, the sculptor, and the teacher. But there are only two instances in which this sharing in divine causality deserves to have the name of Fatherhood as it does in God: in the family and in the priesthood.

Now, it is to be remembered that God incorporates others into His plan for running the universe; God utilizes created causes in making the world what it is. This is so not because He needs these created causes; He is not in need of help. He does not utilize these agents for His own good, but for the good of the agents. It is not a question of adding something to Himself, but of adding something to us. It is a matter of sharing His dignity with us. It is an indication of the profundity of His desire to share Himself with the world, of the depth of His desire to pour Himself out into His work, of the length to which He goes in His goodness.

It is in terms of this desire, of this part of the divine plan for creation, that the sacraments of Holy Orders and Matrimony make sense. It is from this point of view that they fit into the divine plan in the same way and have something very important in common. And it is for this reason that both the head of the family and the priest have the same name as God Himself—*Father*.

The whole of creation is made to the image and likeness of God. But man above all other creatures is said to be the image of God. This is because man is more like to God on account of the spirituality of his soul. It might be argued, then, that the angels have a better claim to this eminence since they are more spiritual than we are. St. Thomas says that we are none the less called the image of God because we share an attribute which the angels do not share, namely, generation.

God has given to man a share in the causality which brings other human beings into existence and to the full stature of human perfection. Of course, it is not a question of being an instrument in the creation of another human soul—the creation of each human soul is the immediate work of God alone. But in the creation of man, both body and soul, we are human instruments in the hands of God. We do have a share, a kind of experience that is not given to the angels. Furthermore, of all the animals, human offspring have greater need than all others for care, protection, and education by parents. Some animals are practically independent at the time of birth; most of them attain self-sufficiency in a short while. Animals seem to have a natural endowment that we call instinct which makes learning unnecessary. But man, above all others, needs the help and care of parents, needs the education and advice of father and mother, the love and appreciation of parents. Human offspring are more dependent, and dependent for a longer time, than any other animals. Which means that human parents are parents on a larger scale than any other parents.

It is not a question now of excluding motherhood from the scheme of things, of excluding mother from sharing in the causality of God. Mother is very important. It is only a matter of customs of thinking. We generally think of father as the head of the family, as the prime educator. When we speak of God sharing His Fatherhood with the human father, we really mean this as applying to both the father and the mother.

In the supernatural order, which consists in the life of grace, God has likewise shared His causality and His care with man. It is not just a question of giving good advice. After all, one angel can give good advice to another angel. It is not just a question of giving good example. After all, the best example can sometimes be given by lay people. It is not just a question of holding the candle that gives the light, of pouring the water that does the washing. The priest is not a priest because he preaches a sermon or leads the hymns or baptizes the babies. The priest is a priest because he actually is an instrument, physical and real, of God in bringing the Mystical Body of Christ into being. He is a priest by reason of the real power He has of changing bread and wine into the real

Body of Christ, and of changing sinners into the members of the Mystical Body of Christ. In these actions He is not just an exhorter or a pleader. In these actions He is a living instrument in the hands of God.

Furthermore, in the priesthood is vested the responsibility of caring for and governing that portion of the Mystical Body which lives upon this earth. In the priesthood is vested the responsibility of being Father to members of the Mystical Body who now live in the society which we call the Church. To the priesthood belongs the responsibility of bringing to man this higher life of grace and of nurturing it to maturity.

One might object that many fathers are not married, and many that are married actually have not received the sacrament of Matrimony. Of course, it is true that all priests are ordained. But it is possible to think that the powers of the priesthood could be given without (being) a sacrament. Granted then, that parenthood and priesthood are two ways in which God shares His causality and His Fatherhood with man, it does not follow of necessity that these two functions are sacraments.

There are some officials in society who can be constituted as such by merely giving them the powers. You can make a jailer by giving him the keys to the jail. You can make a clerk by giving him a rubber stamp. You don't have to give a jailer an education and you don't have to give the clerk a course in character development. On the other hand, you can't make a doctor by giving him a scalpel; you have to give him an education.

So, too, with parenthood and priesthood—merely giving to man the physical powers to accomplish the basic functions of those offices is not enough. It is abundantly clear from experience that sex is not enough to make a parent. For this reason, as a matter of fact, laws are provided which postpone marriage until people supposedly have enough knowledge and character to assume the responsibilities of parenthood. There is more than biology to parenthood. It takes psychological powers as well, it takes wisdom, and understanding, and love. So, too, with the priesthood—merely giving man the powers of the priesthood, e.g., of consecrating and forgiving, is not enough to make a man priestly. If he is going to deal with holy things he should deal with them in a holy way. If he does not, experience has clearly established that his powers are for all practical purposes useless. If priests are not good and holy men, their Masses and confessions are as valid as St. Peter's, but their work is fruitless. A bad life, although it does not vitiate the validity of a priest's work, certainly vitiates its efficacy.

It takes special help from God to be a good parent, especially to be a good Christian parent engaged in the process of rearing children of God. It takes infinite patience to put up with a baby. Many a weary father has called upon God for strength as he paced the floor at night with a bawling bundle of joy in his arms. How much more does it require strength from God to bring a child to full Christian maturity. And it takes special help from God to be holy at all. How much more, then, does it require special help from God to be holy as befits a minister of those awesome powers involved in the consecration of the body of the Lord and the binding and loosing of sins! If power corrupts in the natural order among politicians, how much more is God's help required so that the tremendous powers of the priesthood do not corrupt.

All this would be true even if there were no original sin with its consequent ignorance, weakness, and malice in the human personality. How much more so now; for the Christian parent and the priest are children of Adam. They are as weak, they are as prone to evil as any other child of Adam. But unlike just any other child of Adam they are attempting to do work that is superhuman.

Finally, dignities have a tendency to rest too lightly on human shoulders. Of course, upon being elected to office, everybody, from the local dog catcher to the president, announces that they are unworthy of the great dignity which has been conferred upon them. They promise to be mindful of their dignity all through their term of office and to discharge their duties with the greatest sense of humility and duty. But if there is anything that officials lose faster than their peace and tranquillity of mind, it is their humility. A crown can become as commonplace to a king as shoes to a commoner. A miter can become as commonplace to a bishop as a new hat to a housewife.

If men are to have a permanent sense of dignity they need a special help from God. That is what is provided by making fatherhood and priesthood into sacraments. By a special consecration, by a special act of God which sets these functions aside as holy things, this sense of dignity and vocation is taught to man.

Every man who is called "Father" ought to always remember that He shares that name with God.

water and wine

Since the time of Adam, men about to marry
have taken a ribbing. Since the time of Adam,
though, men who have married have found that
marriage is no laughing matter. As a matter of fact,
marriage is one of the things we sometimes joke
about precisely because it is so serious. And if we
want to find out about marriage we go to serious
men: to psychologists, economists, judges, lawyers, and theologians. Marriage is so serious that
no one profession has all the answers.

Nowadays, we think of the psychologists as
having most of the answers. But the psychologist
has the answers only to psychological problems—
for instance, what a husband should do with a
wife who spends more than he makes, and what
a wife should do with a husband who does not
appreciate home cooking. Economists are valu-
able in that they provide clues on how two can

live as cheaply as one—an economic myth that traps many an unsuspecting couple. Judges and lawyers have in our times come into prominence as marriage counselors, but mainly as the arrangers for or dissuaders from divorce.

What, then, is the theologian's contribution to information on marriage? He is interested in marriage precisely as it is a sacrament. The mysteries of imbuing wives with frugality and husbands with appreciation are profound, and their explanations priceless. The technique of reconciling embattled and embittered spouses is a gift but little inferior to miracle working. Yet, however ambitious it may sound, the contribution of the theologian, which is to make clearer the meaning of the sacrament, is of much greater importance to the Christian than all the psychological and legal advice of the experts put together. People are incoherent if they do not know what words mean. People are unhappy if they do not know what marriage means. What dictionaries do for words, the theologian does with marriage. He explains its meaning.

Theologians hold that Christ accomplished the establishment of Matrimony as a sacrament at the marriage feast of Cana. He blessed it in the first place by His presence. And the miracle which Christ worked on that occasion is most appropriate as an example of how He elevated marriage to the dignity of a sacrament. Water, of its very nature, has inherent properties that make it appropriate for slaking thirst. It is invariably wet and frequently cool. However, it is colorless and tasteless and does nothing but simply slake thirst. As a beverage it is at the bottom of the list. By a miracle Jesus changed water into wine, and good wine, too. One might say that He elevated the water to a new dignity. Wine, like water, is invariably wet and frequently cool. It has everything that water has and something more. It is far from colorless, odorless, and tasteless. It not only slakes thirst but delights. It does the same job that water does but in a much finer manner. In this miracle Jesus improved upon the natural properties of water and promoted the liquid in question to a nobler goal.

Thus, too, He dealt with marriage when He made it a sacrament. He improved on the natural properties that marriage has from the hand of God who is the Author of nature, and promoted it to a nobler goal. The elevation of Matrimony to a sacrament does for natural marriage what the miracle of Cana did for water. The full import of this elevation requires that we have a knowledge of the natural properties of marriage in the first place, and that we have a knowledge of the nobler goal to which Christ directed this institution.

First, consider sex and marriage as a natural institution, as the matter into which Christ breathed the soul of grace which made it a sacrament. Adam and Eve were created as man and wife; they were not first created and then married. God wanted Adam to have a wife so He created Eve. A wife for Adam was not an afterthought. In other words, in terms of Divine Revelation, sex and marriage are corelative ideas and one is inexplicable without the other. Marriage is the explanation of sex just as music is the explanation of a violin.

The most important thing to know about man is his goal or destiny, that he was made to know and love God in this life and be happy with Him forever in heaven. And the most important thing to know about sex and marriage is its goal or purpose. One learns best of man's destiny by inquiring into the purposes God had in mind when He created man. One learns best of the purpose of sex and marriage by inquiring into the idea that God had in mind in inventing them.

God created man in the first place out of an abundance of joy in being God. The creation of man was an overflow of divine happiness. He made man to His own image and likeness that man might be able to share, at least in a small way, in the experience of divine happiness. Remember that God's happiness or beatitude consists in knowing Himself. Likewise man's happiness consists in knowing God. It was because of this that God invented man's immortal soul and the human intellect and will. Now the physical and psychological differences between men and women that make marriage possible are also a divine invention. They have the same motivation behind their invention as do intellect and will. Sex is in the human species an agency for sharing in Godliness. It is meant by God to be an instrument whereby He shares with us the characteristic of creativity. Man the parent is a thousand times closer to the creativity of God than man the artist. Furthermore, God invented sex and marriage as a way in which the divine experience of love could be shared. All creation is patterned after God. And in a special way human love is patterned after divine love; its beauty is a faint reflection of the beauty of divine love. Hence, sex is also an instrument whereby human love is expressed and increased.

When God created Adam and Eve as husband and wife, He arranged that they were to share His creativity relative to their children in the fullest degree possible, from microscopic beginning to full maturity. Their children were not to be finished products, fully developed in the first instant of their being. Rather, their children were to be the fruit of years of creativity involving the totality of their parents' energies, the full impact of their total personalities both physical and spiritual. The whole of Adam and Eve were to be involved in this creative act on a long term basis. And the totality of their children's nature was to depend upon the parents, body and soul. Of course, man can have no share in the actual creation of the human soul of his children and can act only indirectly on those souls in the process of forming character. The completeness of this sharing in divine creativity involves the permanent relationship in family life that we call marriage. It precludes such casual relationships of man and woman as are possible between partners in a bridge game. For parenthood requires a mutual and total effort.

As a matter of fact, God associated the two functions of sex in such a way that they are organically and dynamically integrated. As far as God is concerned, He arranged that children should be conceived in an act of love. In God's plan, sex is so arranged that it simultaneously and in one single act achieves both its goals, i.e., to share in divine creativity and in divine love. Thus human nature, with its capacities for love and understanding, with its physical and psychological sexual differences, united by a solemn contract involving one man and one woman, is adequate to the job of promoting mutual love and rearing self-sufficient and mature members of the human race. Human nature as God made it, sex as God made it, and marriage as God made it are three ingredients necessary for the achievement of the double goal, which is a share in the divine attributes of creativity and love. This is the natural institution, which Jesus used to make a new sacrament. He elevated this arrangement to the dignity of a sacrament by adding one more element—grace—and by promoting the institution to more noble goals.

As far as the first goal of marriage is concerned —marriage considered as a natural arrangement— it should terminate in the generation and education of naturally perfect human characters, of children who have been born and educated and who have matured to the level of self-sufficiency and responsibility. It is not quite right to say that the first end of marriage is children; it would be better to say that the primary goal of marriage is adults. In elevating marriage to the dignity of a sacrament, Jesus did not abolish this goal but rather advanced it one step further. Marriage as a sacrament has not only self-sufficient citizens as its goal, but saints for the kingdom of heaven; not only naturally perfect adults, but supernaturally perfect Christians; not only members of the human race, but members of the Mystical Body of Christ.

As far as the second goal of marriage is concerned—again considered as a natural arrangement—marriage should terminate in the abiding and mutual love of husband and wife. Discounting for the moment the tragic results of the lack of virtues, marriage as a natural arrangement should provide the instrumentality whereby husband and wife progressively grow in their affection for one another. As Heywood Broun put it, "marriage is the best way for two people to get acquainted." But when Jesus elevated marriage to the dignity of a sacrament He established as its goal, not just perfect human love between man and wife, but divine love or charity. The pattern or the type of this new kind of love which marriage should achieve is the bond of love which exists between Christ and the Church. Thus St. Paul writes to the Ephesians:

Be subject to one another in the fear of Christ. Let wives be subject to their husbands as to the Lord; because a husband is head of the wife, just as Christ is head of the Church, being himself savior of the body. But just as the Church is subject to Christ, so also let wives be to their husbands in all things.

Husbands, love your wives, just as Christ also loved the Church, and delivered himself up for her, that he might sanctify her, cleansing her in the bath of water by means of the word; in order that he might present to himself the Church in all her glory, not having spot or wrinkle or any such thing, but that she might be holy and without blemish. Even thus ought husbands also to love their wives as their own bodies. He who loves his own wife, loves himself. For no one ever hated his own flesh; on the contrary he nourishes and cherishes it, as Christ also does the Church (because we are members of his body, made from his flesh and from his bones).

"For this cause a man shall leave his father
and mother,
and cleave to his wife;
and the two shall become one flesh."

This is a great mystery—I mean in reference to Christ and to the Church. However, let each one of you also love his wife just as he loves himself; and let the wife respect her husband (5:21-33).

By reason of charity "thou shalt love thy neighbor as thyself"; i.e., we are to wish for our neighbor the same supernatural blessedness that we wish for ourselves. "For the love of God"—this phrase assigns not the measure, not the benefit intended, but the motive for the love we are to have as the children of God; we must remember that God wishes all His children to share in His blessedness. Charity thus reaches new realms of selflessness. The only example St. Paul can think of that is concrete and convincing is the example of the bond of love that exists between Christ and the Mystical Body. Thus, the sacrament of Matrimony not only builds up the Mystical Body in the sense of providing material members for it, but also in the sense of cementing the bonds that exist between two particular members of that Body. What the Eucharist does for all the parts of the Mystical Body, the sacrament of Matrimony is supposed to accomplish in a special way for man and wife.

Even without original sin and its effects upon human nature, being a parent and a spouse would be a difficult accomplishment. If rearing noble characters and good citizens is a difficult job, rearing saints is well-nigh impossible. If being a good wife and husband is a difficult job, reincarnating the love and devotion of Christ and the Church is an achievement beyond the power of mere human nature. For this reason, Christ made Matrimony a sacrament, i.e., a source of grace. He added one more ingredient to the formula for successful family life, and it is the most important ingredient of all.

A sacrament is an outward sign of inward grace, instituted by Christ. Marriage is an external reality. The actual contract of marriage is as external as any contract, and the married state itself is a concrete and visible thing. As a natural thing created by God, it is filled with significance. For example, Eve, the first wife, came from the side of Adam. This was a prefiguring of the origin of the Church from Christ. The Fathers of the Church were quick to see the analogy fulfilled on Calvary when blood and water came from the side of Christ: the blood a sign of the Eucharist and the water a sign of Baptism—the two sacraments whereby the Church comes into existence and is fostered. Thus by reason of the sign, i.e., Eve from the rib of Adam, the sacrament of Matrimony points to the death of Christ as the origin of its sacramental graces. It also points to the union of Christ and the Church as the goal to which it tends by using this grace.

When the stag parties and bridal showers are over, one Christian man and one Christian woman stand before a priest of God and hear the words: "My dear friends, you are about to enter into a union which is most sacred and most serious." No adjectives could better describe the situation.

True, Christian marriage proposes to bride and groom goals that are freighted with eternal consequences for immortal souls, goals which make "companions of the cupboard" dynamic agents in the Mystical Body of Christ and sharers to the full of the creative prerogatives of God. But with responsibilities go a sense of accomplishment and vocation. The bulk of married life involves drudgery—scrubbing thousands of acres of floors, washing millions of dishes and clothes, cooking endless hundreds of meals, cashing thousands and thousands of pay checks. Only love and a sense of vocation can make all these experiences meaningful. In a civilization whose only goal is comfort, only theological insight can give meaning to the sacrifices that marriage involves. Only those who can read the "sign" can enjoy the cup to the full.

The ministers of this sacrament are the groom and the bride. The priest is only one of three official ecclesiastical witnesses. This is the only time in life that most Catholics become involved in the sacramental system of Christ as ministers, as givers of grace. They are ministers, not only when they stand before the altar of God, but ministers of this sacrament throughout all the days of their married life. This is the one sphere of life where most Christian men and women become sharers in the plans of God in an intimate and active way.

Marriages have always been occasions of joy. They should be. Honestly entered upon they are the life of society. And Christian marriages, especially, should be occasions of joy. Honestly entered upon, they are the life of the Mystical Body of Christ. There is no room for water at a Christian wedding.

chapter fifteen

graceful exit

Usually the sacrament of Extreme Unction, or last anointing, is considered as a sort of spiritual medicine. There are some grounds for this view. It is based on the fact that in ancient times oil was used as a medicine, and on the fact that this sacrament is given only to the sick and decrepit. It is also based on the fact that friends and relatives frequently call in the priest after doctors have given up hope, for a secondary effect of this sacrament is to restore health to the body if that be God's will.

In this chapter, however, the sacrament of last anointing is going to be considered as a masterpiece in the art of consoling. The analogy from the art of medicine is well-founded and has behind it the weight of tradition. The analogy from the art of consoling is also well-founded. It is based on the Council of Trent which says that this sacrament "alleviates and confirms the soul of the sick man by exciting in him great confidence in the divine mercy." This analogy also seems to express more fully the point of view of the medieval theologians in their appreciation of this sacrament.

Anyone who has ever tended the sick or stood around the bed of the dying knows that there is a world of difference between giving medicine and giving consolation. The difference is even plainer to the person on the other end of the thermometer. It is the difference between a bitter pill and the touch of a friendly hand, between hygienic efficiency on the part of a stranger and a familiar smile. Medicine helps our sickness. Consolation helps our wretchedness. Medicine can be learned out of a book and administered by strangers. Consolation is a more delicate art and can be best administered by someone we love and admire. Make no mistake! Consoling is a special art. Sometimes the sick man needs just a bit of cheering up but a bad joke would definitely be the wrong thing. Once the doctor has one in stitches, fumbling jokesters are unwelcome. And the deeper and more profound the wretchedness is, the harder it is to find the right word, the right gesture that will do some good. As a matter of fact, this art is so rare that usually the best thing that friends and relatives can do is stay away.

When a Christian begins to realize that either because of sickness or old age there is a better than fifty-fifty chance that death will come soon, like all other men he becomes a very wretched person. When it becomes no longer possible to stall off the thought of death, as we all do day in and day out; when the thought "my earthly life is coming to an end soon, very soon, any day now, any minute now"; when that thought settles grimly upon a Christian, he has good reason to feel very wretched. In many ways his psychological predicament is worse than the pagans. Unlike the pagan, he has both a past and a future to worry about.

When one faces death as a sick man or as an old man, he faces death as a weak man. And the sicker he is and the older he is, the weaker he is. Sickness and old age sap one's strength, not only one's physical strength—the power to walk and talk, but also one's spiritual strength—the power to think clearly and to will firmly. As death comes closer this power becomes weaker and weaker. It is either a case of pain shrieking louder and louder and drowning out all thoughts and personal feelings, stimulating with the power of an avalanche or a waterfall the desire to escape from consciousness and responsibility; or it is a case of relentless waves of anaesthesia wafting over one's senses and lulling one away from the shores of life. But whatever shape it may take, the spiritual powers of concentration and volition get weaker and weaker.

Remember, too, that death is not just a biological occurrence. It is a psychological experience. And, unlike a sneeze, it happens only once. If one feels a sneeze coming on one knows what the experience is going to be like. In private one might even anticipate it with some delight. But when death comes on, one does not know what it is going to be like. It will be a strange and new experience. All that will be clear about this event is that it is going to be permanent, and that it is going to put an end to human existence as we have known it, that everything familiar is going to cease.

Unlike the pagan, the Christian knows that in this moment he is supposed to commend himself completely to God, that he is supposed to suffer death willingly as the price for original sin. To face death as Christ faced it is perhaps the most tremendous act of virtue that a man shall ever be called upon to make, for everything within him recoils from it and no experience has prepared him for it. And in that awful moment of death all the powers of hell will make their last tremendous bid for the Christian soul. This is indeed a wretched moment for the Christian. Nature leaves him at his weakest. Faith demands the utmost.

The dying Christian feels wretched with depression and uneasiness about his past. Grant that he has been to confession and that the burden of guilt has been removed from his soul. But we all have the uneasy suspicion, and the dying Christian has the uneasy certitude, that God expects great things of us, that He expects us to be not just mediocre, luke-warm Christians, but thorough-going imitators of Christ, real saints. Better than anyone else, the dying Christian knows that Christ is the yardstick against which He measures us. The dying Christian knows with an undeniable awareness that God gives opportunities and graces to every man to be a saint. Yet the dying Christian, however conscientious he may have been, is conscious with an indisputable insight that he has failed to live up to divine expectations; that from neglect, or from being over much occupied with money-making, or family worries, or pleasure seeking, or housekeeping, or from just plain half-heartedness, he has disappointed His Maker. The Christian life is supposed to be a step-by-step growth in charity. It is supposed to involve maturing in body and in soul. And when life is spent and death is at hand, all one's sins, all one's wasted opportunities, all one's failures to grow in love weigh down upon one. They fill the dying Christian with uneasiness, with disappointment in self, with depression.

Wretched from weakness, wretched from depression, the dying Christian faces death. Can the touch of any friendly hand, the sound of any friendly voice console him?

Out of the darkness and through the centuries comes the friendly hand of Christ. It traces a cross upon his brow, upon his lips, upon his eyes, upon his hands and feet. And accompanying that hand comes the voice of all the Church; The Mystical

Body of Christ brings to his ears those wondrous words: "Through this holy anointing and His most tender mercy, may the Lord forgive whatever wrongs you have committed."

The natural gesture of consolation is a caress from a friendly hand. And this is one of the very few sacraments in which one feels the touch of the priestly hand, the priestly hand which is armed with the powers of Christ and is an instrument of Christ Himself. This is the hand that has been consecrated to God. This is the hand which holds the Body of the Lord. This is the hand which is forever raised in blessing. By the miracle of the sacrament of Orders, it is a hand which conveys the power which was in the hand that touched and healed the man filled with leprosy. By the miracle of ordination it is the hand which lifted Peter from sinking beneath the waves and brought to life the only son of a widowed mother. In virtue of the priesthood, it is the hand pierced by the nails which brought faith to the doubting Thomas. The touch of no other friendly hand can mean so much.

Just as the priest's hand is not his own but the hand of Christ, so, too, the priest's voice is not his own but the voice of the Mystical Body of Christ. It is the voice that preaches the Gospel, that changes the bread and wine into the Body and Blood of Christ, the voice that speaks with the authority of the Father in heaven in forgiving sins. It is a voice that God never refuses to hear. And when God listens to that voice, He hears the voice of the whole Church, of the whole Mystical Body of Christ, both Head and members. Christ crucified, the angels, and the saints of all the ages in heaven and on the earth lift up their hearts to God when the priest whispers in the ear of the dying Christian, "Through His most tender Mercy may the Lord forgive whatever wrongs you have committed."

The gentle touch of Christ's own hand and the kindly voice of the Church are the perfect gesture of consolation. And by the touch of this hand and in answer to this prayer, God pours into the soul of the dying Christian those special graces which are needed to console him in his wretchedness. When every other hand is helpless, this hand is filled with help. When every other voice is hopeless, this voice is filled with hope. For the grace of last anointing gives a man the strength he needs to face death and all the powers of hell with confidence. It arms him with the strength of Christ. And this grace gives the dying Christian the power to love with the charity of Christ, to love with the love of a saint, to make up for all the retarded spiritual growth of a life-time in one final act of love. In that dread moment there can be no other consolation.

Medieval theologians thought of this sacrament of last anointing as the final stroke in a masterpiece. It was the finishing touch of the Master Artist bringing His work to perfection. It filled out in a moment what might have been lacking in a life-time to make the soul prepared for glory. Whereas sins had been removed by Penance, last anointing took away all the remains of sin, the proneness to evil that makes the soul lethargic and sluggish in the pursuit of love. It purified and healed and accelerated growth. It prepared the soul to face death by preparing the soul to face glory.

For some strange reason, Catholics by and large have failed to appreciate this masterpiece of Christ. They tend to think of the priest standing by the side of the sick bed as the grim reaper and put off phoning him until the last moment; and after looking up his phone number, they will usually check on the undertaker just to make sure. They worry about calling the priest for fear they might bring panic to the sick person. Though sound medical advice is to the contrary, many Catholics seem to think that it is kinder to lie to the sick person and tell him that everything is going to be all right, that he is going to get well and that he has nothing to worry about. They seem to feel that the presence of the priest would give the lie to their lie. Only when lies and hypodermic syringes have failed do they think it is time to call the priest. They call the priest as a last desperate chance for curing the patient after all the doctors have failed.

Nothing could be more horribly wrong. There could be no greater perversion of charity. Human cruelty can reach no crueler depths. If you have any spark of real charity in your hearts and any love at all for those who are sick unto death, do not delay to call the priest as soon as there is danger of death in the proximate future. When our loved ones are in that miserable state, no one but the priest can console them.

Now it is true that one of the secondary effects of this sacrament is to restore health to the body if that be God's will. But to make a secondary effect a primary reason for calling in the priest or receiving this sacrament is a big mistake. It means a person is more in love with this vale of tears than with heaven. It means a person has mistaken the fight for the trophy. The way to receive Extreme Unction is not to accept death and glory as a second best eventuality. Rather it should be more a question of resigning ourselves to recovery. The phrase "if it be God's will" should express more resignation than hope.

Once upon a time there was a good monk who was stricken one afternoon with what appeared to be a stroke. He was anointed by the abbot and his brethren were assembled around his bed awaiting the end. In that solemn moment the doctor arrived and, after a brief examination, diagnosed the monk's ailment as indigestion. The monk broke down and cried with disappointment. The moral of this story is not that we should watch our diet.

Of all the graces which we beg from God, above all else we should ask that when death approaches, out of the enshrouding darkness a priestly hand should come and rest upon our brow and that the voice of the Church should sound in our ears. It will be hard to make a graceful exit without them.